Jamgon Kongtrul's Retreat Manual

Jamgon Kongtrul's Retreat Manual
by Jamgon Kongtrul Lodro Tayé

translated by Ngawang Zangpo

Snow Lion
Boston & London

Snow Lion
An imprint of Shambhala Publications, Inc.
Horticultural Hall
300 Massachusetts Avenue
Boston, Massachusetts 02115
www.shambhala.com

Printed in the United States of America

♾ This edition is printed on acid-free paper that meets the American National Standards Institute Z39.48 Standard.
♻ Shambhala Publications makes every effort to print on recycled paper. For more information please visit www.shambhala.com.
Distributed in the United States by Random House, Inc., and in Canada by Random House of Canada Ltd

Library of Congress Cataloging-in-Publication Data

Koṅ-sprul Blo-gros-mtha'-yas, 1813–1899.
Jamgon Kongtrul's retreat manual / by Jamgon Kongtrul; translated by Ngawang Zangpo (Hugh Leslie Thompson).
p. cm.
Includes bibliographical references.
ISBN 978-1-55939-029-3
1. Spiritual life—Bka'-rgyud-pa (Sect). 2. Spiritual life—Tantric Buddhism. I. Title.
BQ7679.6.K65 1994
294.3'4446—dc20
94-2483
CIP

Table of Contents

Jamgon Kongtrul's Retreat Manual

Dedicated to my teacher, Kalu Rinpochay, whose love, wisdom, and creative spirit have proven to be inexhaustible treasures.

Preface

Jamgon Kongtrul's Retreat Manual has been a valued companion of mine for almost fifteen years. I was introduced to it during a meditation training program modelled on the one described in this text, a three-year, three-fortnight retreat. I completed two such retreats. During those years Kongtrul's words often inspired me, although I never felt equal to the expectations he had for his retreatants. Reading his advice now for those who have finished the retreat continues to be a similarly humbling experience.

The three-year, three-fortnight retreat constitutes one of the central institutions of tantric Buddhist education in the Himalayan region. Within two of the four main monastic networks, the Nyingma and the Kagyu, only those who have completed such retreats receive the title of lama. While programs of training differ from one retreat center to another, this book presents a complete view of one program designed by the author, a well-known and respected meditation master of the nineteenth century. This work should thus provide the basis for an understanding of the many parallel institutions that still furnish training for persons to become "lamas."

Jamgon Kongtrul's Retreat Manual was written to provide a guide to persons entering a three-year intensive meditation program. The author does not accompany his words of counsel with instructions in how to meditate; he simply lists the meditations that comprise the retreat program. The translation of this work has been supplemented by some details about the sources of the meditations mentioned, but no information concerning the content of the visualizations has been included. Instruction in tantric meditation, whether in Kongtrul's time or now, remains within the domain of the relationship a meditator has with his or her trusted spiritual advisor. The same is true for the decision to embark upon a long retreat. This book gives a clear picture of the spiritual and practical life of this kind of institution but this translation was not undertaken with the intention of encouraging the reader to consider entering such a retreat.

I hope that this book will contribute to our knowledge of the non-sectarian view within Himalayan tantric Buddhism and to our appreciation of the author, Jamgon Kongtrul. Both of these important subjects have not yet received the attention they deserve in any language other than Tibetan. A brief account of Kongtrul's life and thought as they concern the retreat is presented in the introduction, including translated quotations from Kongtrul himself. Some of these are quite long but I hope the reader will appreciate the opportunity to read some of Kongtrul's reflections in his own words. There is much more to Kongtrul's life and work than is mentioned here and much more to be said about the non-sectarian movement. No writer can do justice to a person's life in just a few words, let alone the life of such a multi-faceted genius as Kongtrul. In describing his life so briefly, and mainly in relation to the subject matter of this book, I have taken the risk of unintentionally distorting his thought. At the very least this risk will have been worthwhile if my limitations provoke others to present a more detailed picture of Kongtrul to non-Tibetan-speaking readers.

Understanding Kongtrul seems more crucial now than a decade ago because many of the great masters who were his spiritual heirs have recently passed away. The long list includes some who were instrumental in bringing Buddhism to countries outside the Himalayan region: His Holiness Karmapa, His Holiness Dujom Rinpochay, Dilgo Kyentsay Rinpochay, Day-zhung Rinpochay, Pawo Rinpochay, Salchay Rinpochay, Chögyam Trungpa Rinpochay, and my principal teacher who was an incarnation of Kongtrul, Kalu Rinpochay. These masters were trained in Kongtrul's ecumenical style, taught with his gentle but authoritative voice, and continued his work of impartially furthering the development of all forms of Buddhist practice. Because many present-day Buddhists have been profoundly influenced by these masters, their absence forces us to renew our consideration of the source of much of their instruction: Jamgon Kongtrul.

This book is concerned first and foremost with the three-year, three-fortnight retreat, an institution vital to Himalayan tantric

Buddhism. Nonetheless, it was not coincidental to my choice of text to translate that this retreat was central to Kongtrul's life and a showcase for his non-sectarian ideal.

NOTES ON THE STYLE OF THE TRANSLATION

This translation is not intended to be innovative or challenging in style. I have occasionally departed from conventional norms in minor ways, usually in preference for English words over their Sanskrit or Tibetan equivalents. Where foreign words remain in the text, they represent my limits as a translator.

Names of persons have been left in their original form, i.e., the name the person was known by during his or her lifetime. This represents a departure from the convention among Tibetan authors, which is to translate most Indian names and render them in Tibetan. I asked three outstanding masters concerning this matter and received three different answers in reply. One master, Dabzang Rinpochay (since deceased), felt that all names of Indian persons or of buddhas, bodhisattvas, and deities should be retranslated into Sanskrit in English translations. Another, Trangu Rinpochay, quoted from a text giving advice to the early Tibetan translators in support of his feeling that whatever can be translated, all names included, should be rendered in English. While I am personally sympathetic to that opinion, I have here followed the advice of the third master I questioned, Tai Situpa. He declared that the Tibetan translators were wrong to translate the names of persons: these should not be translated. Buddhas, bodhisattvas, and deities' names should be translated, he said, as these are not human individuals. I sincerely respect all three of these masters; their opinions are important to me. I have chosen to follow Tai Situpa's advice because it seems the most practical at the present time. I hope the result will not prove disorienting for those accustomed to being served large mouthfuls of Sanskrit with their Buddhism. A list of the names that appear in the main text of the retreat manual can be found at the end of the book.

Books cited in the introduction or in the main text appear with an English title. Unfortunately very few of these have been translated from Tibetan into any foreign language. The Tibetan titles of these books are listed at the end of the book. This information is crucial in identifying the original because Tibetan book-titles often stretch to a couple of lines of text: any translator must decide what portion of the original title, if any, to use as the title in English. For example, the full Tibetan title of this book could be translated as *A Source of Comfort and Cheer: A Clear Guide to the Rules of Discipline for the Retreatants at The Ever-Excellent Abode of Radiant Great Bliss, the Isolated Retreat of Palpung.* Instead of using all or part of this title, the present title seemed both more practical and more descriptive of the book's content. Translators must make these choices; many of the books mentioned in this text with English titles may someday appear with another title entirely.

On the subject of terminology, the reader may notice that I have avoided where possible calling the Buddhism of the Himalayan region "Tibetan" Buddhism. The predominant language of Buddhism in the Himalayas certainly is Tibetan, but many past and present masters and disciples of this form of spiritual development are not Tibetan. These non-Tibetans include Indians, Bhutanese, Nepalese, Sikkimese, and members of many other ethnic and linguistic groups resident throughout the Himalayan region. They share a common faith and use a common language for their prayers and meditations, but many are no more Tibetan than a Roman Catholic is necessarily Italian. Kongtrul, for his part, usually wrote of Buddhism of "the Himalayan region" (*gangs chen rdzong*) rather than of Tibet, and I have been happy to follow his example.

The words *Nyingma, Kagyu, Sakya,* and *Gayluk* are seldom mentioned in this book. I have reserved their use for when Kongtrul seems to be referring to what these four represent: the four main monastic systems of the Himalayan region. In most of his books most of the time, Kongtrul discusses tantric Buddhism of the Himalayan region from the point of view of the lineages of meditation practice, specifically the eight practice lineages. (This is discussed more fully in the introduction.) The names of these lineages of meditation instruction appear in English within this book, despite unavoidable shortcomings in the translations. For example, the Marpa Kagyu lineage is rendered here as the Oral Instruction Lineage of Marpa, whereas the word *Kagyu* is a contraction of a rarely used name, Kabab Shi'i Gyupa — the Instruction Lineage of the Four Transmissions, a reference to part of the lineage's origins. As inaccurate as it might be, however, "Oral Instruction Lineage" is found in this text, and this is certainly not the first time such a translation has been used.

The word *lama* appears very frequently in the Tibetan text but seldom in the translation. This word in Tibetan can refer to any graduate of the three-year retreat or to an enlightened master who is capable of guiding a person through all the stages of spiritual development to full and complete enlightenment. My own teacher used to remark that the former kind of lama was quite common, the latter exceedingly rare. While the same word for both is used in Tibetan, "lama" appears in the translation when Kongtrul is referring to retreat graduates, and "spiritual master" when he is referring to an enlightened spiritual guide, male or female.

I have been perplexed with how to treat Kongtrul's habit of calling tantric Buddhism "Secret Mantra," not a fashionable term among modern Buddhists. I decided to put my own preferences aside and to be faithful to Kongtrul's style, as odd or even distasteful as "Secret Mantra" might sound to our ears.

Within the retreat manual, introductory sections have been inserted which give background information and historical context for the practices to be discussed. In order to better distinguish these from the main text of the retreat manual, the introductory sections have been printed in a smaller type size.

Finally, in the footnotes, the Tibetan equivalent of a term is sometimes provided within brackets. The first word or phrase that appears in non-italicized type is an approximate pronunciation of the Tibetan word. This is followed by the actual Tibetan spelling in italics.

ACKNOWLEDGEMENTS

This translation has benefitted at various stages from the assistance or suggestions of a number of persons. Lama Tsondru and Lama Umdzay Zopa, both graduates of the retreat center described in this book when it was under the guidance of Kalu Rinpochay, were particularly helpful in untying some of the knots of Kongtrul's colloquial style. Yudra Tulku, Khamtrul Rinpochay, Geshe Sonam Rinchen, Zenkar Rinpochay (through Peter Roberts), Dr. Tenpa Kelzang, and Nyima Tenzin Bashi also contributed to my understanding of the Tibetan text. They have all done their best to ensure this text is error-free: mistakes that remain are due entirely to the translator. Lama Drubgyu Tenzin (Tony Chapman) gave me invaluable support and encouragement with the English version of this book. I am also thankful for the comments and criticisms of Kitty Rogers, Lama Kunzang Dorjay (Olivier Brunet), and Michael Rey.

I have made use of the computer facilities at the International Buddhist Translation Committee of Sonada, India, and of the considerable patience of my colleagues there toward my absenteeism during my work on this book. I am grateful for both.

Finally, Faye Angevine of Taipei and Lama Gyaltsen of Sonada Monastery supported me materially during my work on this translation. Their generosity has been timely and is deeply appreciated. I am equally indebted to the Hirota family of Tokyo, who kindly sponsored my journey to Kongtrul's retreat center in Kham where I found the answers to many of my questions.

Translator's Introduction

This translation of *Jamgon Kongtrul's Retreat Manual* is intended as a modest contribution to our understanding of meditation training in the tantric tradition of Buddhism and of the life of the author, a nineteenth-century meditation master whose work remains one of the dominant influences in modern Himalayan tantric Buddhism.

This short book was written as a guide for those entering an intensive three-year meditation training program. The author, director of the program, advises his students how to prepare for the retreat, what will be expected of them during their stay in his center, and how to lead their lives upon the successful completion of their training.

If we find the subject of meditation training in a retreat daunting or mysterious to begin with, this is not due to any innate difficulty of the subject itself: we simply do not have any parallel to it within non-Buddhist cultures. This book gives us practically unlimited access to the closed world of a retreat. The view afforded by this small window has not been cosmeticized. It is doubtful that the author ever expected this work would be examined by a readership so far removed from his own culture and time. Intentionally or not, however, he gives modern readers the most accurate, de-mystified portrait possible of this kind of institution.

A major section of this book is devoted to a detailed description of the program of the retreat. This information is particularly noteworthy in the case of Jamgon Kongtrul ("Gentle Protector") (1813-99), as it reveals his personal interests and preferences within the wide range of Buddhist meditation practices.

During the nineteenth century, Kongtrul was responsible for the compilation of *The Five Treasuries* that contain the best of over a thousand years of Tibetan-speaking people's experience of the study of Buddhism and the practice of its meditations. In all, these five collections comprise over one hundred volumes of 400 to 800 pages each (using a Western numbering system). Of these, approximately thirty volumes are of Kongtrul's original work that supplements and elucidates the works of past meditation masters.

It would be difficult to overestimate the influence these books have had. They are the format in which many modern Tibetan-speaking Buddhists continue to receive their spiritual inheritance. They are universally respected as a major source of the authoritative and reliable guides to study and meditation needed for spiritual development within Buddhism.

Unfortunately, non-Tibetan-speaking readers have little access to this man and his work. Only two translations of his books have appeared in English: *The Great Path of Awakening* and *The Torch of Certainty*. Both are careful and accurate translations, faithful to the author's style. But they represent two very small drops drawn from an ocean. In the Tibetan original the former is 46 pages long; the portion of the latter that was published in English, 101 pages. The original Tibetan volume of which they are both a part contains 758 pages in all and is itself just one of over one hundred volumes of Kongtrul's original works and his compilations. *Jamgon Kongtrul's Retreat Manual* (64 pages in Tibetan) is nothing more than another tiny taste from a particularly copious banquet.

The special significance of this book in understanding Jamgon Kongtrul derives from the central place the retreat center described here occupied in his life. The Ever-Excellent Abode of Radiant Great Bliss, as the center was known, was Jamgon Kongtrul's principal place of residence for most of his long life. He wrote most of his books there, often initially for the use of the retreatants. His care with every aspect of life within retreat that we sense in this book is a clue to the fact that this was the only such center he founded. This was his home and it was entirely his own — from the physical structure and its contents to the meditation practices done by the retreatants. By reading his counsel to his students, who were in a real way guests in his physical home and his spiritual world, we can glimpse what Jamgon Kongtrul held most dear.

The following introduction furnishes some general information concerning the two main subjects of this book: the three-year meditation retreat as an institution and the importance of this retreat in the life and work of Jamgon Kongtrul.

THE THREE-YEAR, THREE-FORTNIGHT RETREAT

RETREAT CENTERS: THEIR PHYSICAL SETTING

In the Buddhist scheme of spiritual development, study and reflection find their consummation in meditation. While a close connection between study and meditation is considered ideal in theory, the two trainings are usually separated institutionally. Budding scholars gravitate to monastic colleges; future master meditators enter retreat centers, the institution designed to impart a thorough training in meditation.

In the traditions of the Ancient Instruction Lineage (Nyingma) and the Oral Instruction Lineage (Kagyu), the basic intensive meditation training program lasts three years and three fortnights. *Jamgon Kongtrul's Retreat Manual* was written as a guide to this style of retreat. No standard model exists for the physical structure of these retreat centers. The following description is based on retreat centers I have visited in the Himalayan region — Tibet, India, and Nepal — and in foreign countries — France, Canada, and Taiwan.

A meditation retreat center usually stands apart from the main grounds of a monastery, temple, or public meditation center. Retreats are self-sufficient micro-communities served and protected by the larger institution to which they are affiliated.

Seen from the exterior, retreat centers are islands of stillness: they are not meant to draw attention to themselves. Persons entering retreat leave any duties and responsibilities to family, livelihood, or society at the door, to be re-assumed after their chosen period of training has been completed. Members of the public are not permitted to enter the retreat at any time during the program. The only persons leaving or entering the retreat compound during the retreat period are the attendant-cook and designated meditation instructors.

Within the retreat enclosure a number of buildings encircle a courtyard. Each retreatant has a room of his or her own and it is there that the meditator spends most of the day. The largest building is a temple where the whole community gathers twice daily — morning and evening — for group prayers and meditation. (Breakfast and supper are served at these times in retreats in the Himalayan region.) Also within the enclosure is a large room for yoga exercises. The other structures within the retreat house the kitchen, washroom, and toilet. The whole area is closed to the public's eyes by walls or fences.

Each retreatant's room affords just enough space for a small shrine, some bookshelves, a reading table and a place for the occupant to stretch out on the floor in a gesture of prostration. Each room's window opens onto the inner courtyard. Instead of a bed, the rooms are furnished with a "meditation seat," a wooden support which has three low sides and a high back. This serves as both a meditation seat and a bed: participants in long-term intensive retreats (such as the one for which this manual was written) must habituate themselves to sleeping in a seated, upright position.

Retreat centers are commonly small communities, often numbering a dozen resident meditators or less. Monasteries and monastic colleges in the Himalayan region have a certain notoriety for tending to the grandiose. Not so retreat centers: a healthy teacher-student ratio is always considered essential in such communities. For example, only eight persons made up the retreat community in Jamgon Kongtrul's retreat: one master, five retreatants, one cook, and one woodsman.

Jamgon Kongtrul's retreat center departed from the conventional model in a few minor ways. There was more than one temple within the enclosure and two programs of meditation were followed concurrently within the one retreat community. The second program was followed by the one retreatant responsible for the second temple, dedicated to the Buddhist protectors. Unlike most modern meditation centers, the residents of this retreat had to leave all their personal possessions in storage for the duration of the retreat. This constraint later became all-inclusive, from religious articles (such as statues and paintings) to clothes: in later retreats, even the one-size-fits-all monastic robes were provided by the center. This enforced conformity would seem to underline Jamgon Kongtrul's insistence that the meditators in his center were to see themselves and to be treated as equals, regardless of their wealth or social standing outside the retreat.

THE TIME PERIOD OF THE RETREAT

The program of Jamgon Kongtrul's retreat was squeezed very tightly into a three-year, three-fortnight period. This might seem both arbitrary and inconvenient; however, it follows a tradition that began long before Kongtrul's time.

In the year before his death, the Buddha taught *The Tantra of the Wheel of Time (Kalachakra)*, said to represent the pinnacle of his instructions. In this tantra the Buddha describes the relationship between the universe, time, and one's own body. His presentation provides the rationale for determining the optimum length of a meditation retreat as three years and three fortnights.

Briefly, our most fundamental relationship with the outside world after birth is through the breath. We breathe: we live. Moreover, according to *The Tantra of the Wheel of Time,* our breathing is naturally linked to the universe and to time. In *The Encyclopedia of Buddhism,* Kongtrul states:

> Externally there are twenty-one thousand, six hundred minutes in one year [of 360 days], while internally this is the number of breaths taken daily. (Volume 2, page 639)

The air we breathe enters our bodies and sustains the life-force we have in common with all beings, called karmic energy. According to the tantric view, a small portion of the breath also sustains our spiritual potential, called wisdom energy. Kongtrul states:

> One thirty-second of each breath is wisdom energy.... Its nature is the indestructible enlightened mind. (*ibid,* Volume 2, pages 639-40)

This one thirty-second of each breath that nurtures our spiritual potential is, by definition, a minor part of normal life. Its influence is curtailed by the attention we give to "real life," i.e., karmic energy. Time spent in meditation retreat greatly diminishes the force of karmic energy. Ideally, all the work, the drives, the emotions, and the habits or lifestyles that dominate our lives in the world are left outside the retreat and supplanted by wisdom energy — the experience of the mind's natural spacious stillness, bliss, and clarity. Less and less of each breath taken sustains karmic energy; instead it enhances wisdom energy. This process culminates in enlightenment, the complete transformation of karmic energy into wisdom energy.

In tantric Buddhism, the human lifespan at the present time is said to be one hundred years. That is to say, our bodies can potentially last that length of time. The one thirty-second of each breath that is wisdom energy, accumulated over that period, is equivalent to the breaths taken in three years and three fortnights. This is said to be the minimum amount of time necessary to complete the transformation of karmic energy to wisdom energy, that is, to achieve complete enlightenment. This state is symbolized by a form of the Buddha known as Vajra Holder (Vajradhara). As Kongtrul states:

> All the wisdom energy which circulates [with the breath] during one hundred years equals three years and three

> fortnights. When all karmic energy is transformed into wisdom energy, enlightenment is attained. This is the reason why it is said that the state of the Buddha Vajra Holder is achieved [by meditation practice during a period of] three years and three fortnights. (*ibid*, Volume 2, page 640)

Retreats such as the one described in this manual are often referred to in English as three-year, three-month retreats. "Fortnight" may not have come into use because it seems too clumsy for modern English usage, or because it is not really an accurate translation. The Tibetan word for fortnight (chok, *phyogs*) means specifically one half-phase of the moon, from new moon to full moon, or from full to new.

Although the period of the retreat is referred to as three years and three fortnights throughout this work, one could reasonably call it a three-year, three-month retreat. The lunar calendar on which the retreat program is based must be readjusted regularly to make up the minimum of five days lost each year in relation to the solar calendar. Every few years, the Tibetan calendar appears with not twelve but thirteen months of sometimes less, but never more, than thirty days each. These extra months are calculated within the program of meditation so that the retreat is sure to last at least three years and two and a half months, if not more. For example, because both 1989 and 1991 were years of thirteen months, such a retreat beginning in January 1989 would have lasted three years and three and a half months.

RETREAT CENTERS AND GENDER

Most long-term, intensive meditation retreats are sexually segregated. Participants in such retreats accept a period of celibacy as a simplification of life which permits them to devote their full time and attention to their spiritual lives.

Jamgon Kongtrul's retreat, The Ever-Excellent Abode of Radiant Great Bliss, was a meditation center for men. Women numbered among his close students — he mentioned at the end of some books that they were written at the request of one or another of his female disciples — however it seems unlikely that he created a parallel center for women, as it goes unmentioned in his writings as far as I know.

Jamgon Kongtrul was first and foremost a meditator and a writer, not an institution builder. He himself seems to have suffered from his experience within the religious institutions of his day, as will be explained below. This place represented for him a spiritual home and an oasis of sanity. Jamgon Kongtrul's main ambition in life seems to have been to understand the spiritual life of his world and time, to collect whatever was of value of the past, to preserve the treasures that were in danger of being lost, and to make them accessible to future generations through his own writing. To say that he succeeded gloriously in that ambition is not to discount the fact that he seems to have acceded to the norms of his day and neglected to create institutional structures for women's retreats.

Does this suggest that Kongtrul did not take women's participation in and contribution to spiritual life seriously? There seems to be little to substantiate such a view and ample evidence to the contrary. In particular, Kongtrul had a wide range of meditations to choose from for his retreat program but he devoted close to half of it to meditations that originated with two Indian women of the tenth century. As well, one of the practices to be done daily throughout the retreat was the inspiration of a Tibetan woman, and features her as the focal point of the meditation.

Most modern three-year retreats outside of the Himalayan region have facilities for both women and men. The two groups follow the same program and receive equal attention from their instructors. In the Himalayan region, however, the situation is radically different. Women often seem to be considered second-class citizens of the Buddhist world. Large monasteries and monastic colleges costing many thousands of dollars to construct and to operate continue to proliferate. Barely a year goes by without yet another ambitious project being unveiled. Among these, institutions which admit women are virtually non-existent. In the case of three-year retreat programs for women of the Himalayan region, to my knowledge only two masters — Tai Situpa of the Kagyu Lineage and Chadral Rinpochay of the Nyingma Lineage — have established and maintain women's retreats that have a standard of instruction equal to those of men's retreats.

MEDITATION TRAINING IN RETREAT

Despite considerable differences among the programs of meditation followed within retreat centers affiliated with different masters or monasteries, some features are common to all.

The retreatants' day is divided into four periods of individual meditation (early morning, late morning, afternoon, and evening) and two group sessions (in the morning and late afternoon). Spare time is a commodity in short supply: the longest pause during the day coincides with the noon meal. The intensity of the training might seem suffocating unless one reflects that the participants normally spend years eagerly preparing for the opportunity to immerse themselves in such a program.

The four daily sessions are devoted to specific meditations that change at irregular intervals; some meditations are done for days, some for months. The retreat program begins with the most elementary meditations of a particular tradition and progresses gradually through all stages of development until the most profound. All the retreatants are expected to follow the program faithfully in spite of whatever preferences they might have among the many meditations offered. Most retreats would introduce the participants to one tradition of meditation techniques. In Jamgon Kongtrul's retreat, the burden of the program's demands was particularly heavy: he directed a full guided tour through three very distinct styles of tantric meditation and supplemented these practices with instructions from four other lineages.

The daily group sessions and the regularly scheduled special rituals involve a considerable amount of busyness: recitation of prayers, playing of instruments, recitation of mantras, preparation of various offerings, and more, always more, recitation of prayers. To many persons, the retreat's meditation program might appear to be already over-charged without such distractions. In fact, however, for participants who understand the language of the texts and are familiar with the visualizations that are done concurrently, the group rituals can be inspiring and uplifting sources of personal renewal.

What constitutes the training in tantric meditation during such a retreat? It is impossible to answer such a question without providing a short explanation of the Buddhist theory of meditation.

In general, a person practices Buddhist meditation in order to calm the mind and to develop insight into its nature. That insight culminates in awakening and enlightenment. But awakening is not a product of meditation — Buddhism doesn't create enlightenment any more than a mirror creates a face. Effective instruction in Buddhist practice is likened to a mirror that permits a person to see his or her own face, our innate buddha-nature. Much of tantric Buddhist training in meditation consists of simply improving the mind's eyesight.

Buddhism teaches that all beings' deepest nature is an inexhaustible reservoir of wisdom, love, and creative potential. What prevent us from clearly perceiving this, our own nature, are the "four obscurations." The first is our fundamental failure to be completely aware of this nature, called the obscuration of ignorance. Due to this lack of intrinsic self-awareness, we continually create identities for ourselves (an I, a self) and others, called the obscuration of habit, the second obscuration. An example of our tendency to create a self and a world and then to believe in our own projections as real is our spontaneous and pervasive fabrication of self and other in dreams.

Once we have created a self, whether in waking life or in dreams, we become subject to myriad emotions based on our experience. This is the third obscuration, the obscuration of emotions. In Buddhist theory an emotion is judged as negative if it tends to prevent our self-understanding or to lead to selfish and harmful physical or verbal acts. These harmful or selfish acts constitute the last obscuration, the obscuration of negative actions.

Tantric meditation and the program of the retreat are designed to counteract and neutralize these four obscurations. The retreat begins with the preliminary practices — meditations to purify the obscuration of negative acts and to cultivate merit and awareness, to use Buddhist jargon. In slightly plainer language, these practices freshen and enrich the meditator's physical, verbal, and mental experience.

The second stage of tantric meditation concerns what are called creation phase meditations, which neutralize the obscuration of the emotions. During these practices, meditators adopt self-images of enlightened beings, male or female, that personify an awakened and lively state of mind. Obscuring emotions arise from the fertile ground of our ordinary sense of embodiment and enworldment. Creation phase meditations offer in its place a total fabrication of a self and an environment. Fabrications, yes, but very skilful ones. Is it possible to really identify with them? Our minds answer that question every night when we believe entirely in our dreams while we sleep, no matter how outlandish they are. Just as some dreams can affect our minds very deeply no matter how much we tell ourselves, "It was only a dream," so these fabrications gradually counteract our negative emotions by providing an experience of the spaciousness and vitality of awakened mind.

The third stage of tantric meditation, the phase of completion, counteracts the obscuration of habit, our pervasive tendency to create a self and other. Unlike the busy fabrications of the creation phase, these meditations open doors to a view of the mind as it is. They allow the meditator to experience directly the mind's natural creativity, how we continually make something — a self and a world — out of nothing. The meditator also learns to follow the return of the play of mind to its source, boundless and centerless luminosity. In the process, habitual self-other frameworks lose their former solid grip on the meditator's mind.

The final stage of tantric meditation is direct meditation on the nature of mind. This is the antidote to the obscuration of ignorance. These practices do not create this awakened nature. To see our own face, we need a mirror; to see our inner nature, we need the mirror of the spiritual master's instructions. The previous stages of meditative training clear away the clouds from the sky of the mind. This stage does not create a sun but recognizes that it — a radiant awareness — was always present, and allows its light and warmth to fill all space. This awareness dispels any trace of our lack of understanding of our own nature.

These four stages of meditation are repeated three times during Jamgon Kongtrul's retreat: preliminary practices, creation phase meditation, completion phase meditation, and meditation on the nature of mind were taught and practiced in three separate styles. Forms and terminology vary among the various traditions of tantric Buddhism, but these four stages are shared by all.

JAMGON KONGTRUL'S LIFE AND WORK AS RELATED TO THE RETREAT

KONGTRUL'S NON-SECTARIAN VIEW AND HIS RETREAT PROGRAM

Jamgon Kongtrul was successful during his lifetime in popularizing a unifying vision of Buddhism that revitalized the spiritual life of the Himalayan region. Tibetan society had grown accustomed to thinking of Tibetan Buddhism as divided into four main traditions: the Nyingma, Kagyu, Sakya, and Gayluk. This understandable simplification is based on the fact that by the nineteenth century these four represented the dominant religious institutional structures after ten centuries of political power struggles. This short list includes the existing monastic systems but not the scholastic and meditative traditions that provided the inspiration for their establishment.

The original intent of the monasteries had been to provide shelter for the training, both scholastic and meditative, in the systems of spiritual development that had arrived in the Himalayan region from Buddhist India. Over the centuries, however, some monasteries grew beyond mere religious centers: they became petty fiefdoms that wielded temporal power and degenerated into havens for political intrigue and self-serving sectarianism. Kongtrul regarded as spiritually dangerous the interpretation of Buddhist history primarily from the point of view of the development and maintenance of these institutions.

Kongtrul preferred to see the history of spiritual development in the Himalayan region from the point of view of the practice of meditation and the study of philosophy and psychology. In his writing, he always described tantric Buddhism from the perspective of its lineages of instruction; he would mention the four monastic systems only in passing. As one great modern non-sectarian master,

Chögyam Trungpa Rinpochay, succinctly expressed, Kongtrul shifted Buddhists' attention "from the golden roofs of the temples to the meditation cushion."[1] This idea was not new but it took the spiritual authority and skill of Kongtrul and his contemporaries to effectively spread what became known as the *rimay* (*ris med*) — non-sectarian, impartial, or ecumenical — view. The message of this view seems to be that to regard oneself and others primarily as members of religious institutions is to draw artificial barriers between people, as if affiliation to a religious order is equivalent to belonging to a political party. Instead, to see oneself as the practitioner of one or more of the systems of Buddhist spiritual development, all of which share origins and goals, frees one to appreciate the inspiration in them all and thus facilitates communication and co-operation between fellow Buddhist meditators.

This non-sectarian view cut through the stultifying sectarianism and institution-centrism of the day to reach the heart of tantric Buddhist practice: the eight practice lineages. Eight distinct traditions of Indian tantric Buddhist meditation reached the Himalayas during the period of religious exchange between the two regions. It is these eight practice lineages which form the basis of Himalayan tantric Buddhism.[2] Of the eight, only the first shares the name of an existing system of monasteries:

1. Ancient Instruction Lineage (Nyingma, *rnying ma*)
2. Buddha's Word as Instruction Lineage (Kadampa, *bka' gdams pa*)
3. Path and Result Instruction Lineage (Lam Dray, *lam 'bras*)
4. Oral Instruction Lineage of Marpa (Marpa Kagyu, *mar pa bka' brgyud*)
5. Shangpa Instruction Lineage (Shangpa Kagyu, *shangs pa bka' brgyud*)
6. Pacification of Suffering (Sheejay, *zhi byed*) and Severance (Chö, *gcod*) Instruction Lineages
7. Vajra Yoga Instruction Lineage (Dorjay Naljor, *rdo rje rnal 'byor*)

[1] Pages 89-91 of *Journey Without Goal* (Boston: Shambhala, 1981) by Chogyam Trungpa Rinpoche are of particular interest concerning Kongtrul and the non-sectarian movement.

[2] The eight practice lineages (drub gyu shing ta gyay, *sgrub brgyud shing rta brgyad*) are literally the eight chariots or vehicles of the practice lineages. The list given here is that provided by Kongtrul in *The Encyclopedia of Buddhism* and other works. Lists given by other teachers may vary slightly.

8. Intensive Practice of the Three Vajras Instruction Lineage (Dorjay Sum Gyi Nyen Drup, *rdo rje gsum gyi bsnyen sgrub*)

Kongtrul's three-year retreat program was a reflection of his non-sectarian view; teachings from seven of the eight practice lineages are included in it. In the following passage he speaks as a holder of the Oral Instruction Lineage of the Karmapas and mounts an articulate defense of his program based on the history of meditation practice within that lineage. He discusses the subject — what constitutes an effective program of meditation practice — and views it from a number of angles before presenting his conclusion: a well-rounded, impartial exposure to many different styles of meditation constitutes the best solution.

Although he sounds as if he expects to die soon ("I'm now at the end of my life"), he wrote these lines in 1864 (at age 51), at the end of the first three-year retreat at his center. He was to live for another thirty-five years.

> It might seem wisest to focus a three-year, three-fortnight retreat program on just one tradition of creation and completion phase meditations, [having the retreatants] strive diligently to bring those teachings to the point of efficacity. From that point of view, it might seem best if there were not too many elaborate prayers and recitations, as [a simple program] presents fewer difficulties to those of lesser capability and vigor. Nonetheless, some outstanding individuals who have practiced meditation in previous lives appear to be unaffected by the length of time or the degree of effort given to meditation. The inner signs of their complete mastery of the relative and ultimate aspects of the mind of awakening and of the two phases of meditative absorption become manifest through the power of their understanding, love, and ability to help others. Their clear and overt displays [of innate ability] are beyond the scope of ordinary, self-centered individuals.
>
> Due to the deteriorating condition of life these days, most people — including those who have received the name of "realized one" or "accomplished one" after having dedicated years of their lives to meditation and recitation of prayers and mantras — haven't properly taken to heart even [the basic instructions of] the four contemplations which turn the mind to spiritual life[3] and are mostly concerned with the

[3] The four contemplations to turn the mind to spiritual life are

needs of this life. It is therefore extremely rare to find someone who has experience in the two phases of tantric meditation as described in the practice texts. Even if a few persons have developed some fraction of that realization, it seems impossible to find anyone who has enriched his experience beyond this stage.

In general, simple meditation practice on mind alone requires recognition [of its nature], enrichment [of the experience], achievement of stability, and perfection of one's mastery. Without all four of these, one will not achieve one's goal. These days, [meditators] don't progress beyond a very equivocal recognition [of the mind]; their practice is ineffective in times of need, when they find themselves searching for security in divinations, rituals, and the like. This is an example of how one can gradually lose one's firm determination after years of intensively practicing a single meditation. The meditation and one's attention go their separate ways and one becomes completely engrossed in pointless distraction and negative pastimes. Besides the experience one had in meditation, even the faith and the sincere enthusiasm that one had upon beginning meditation practice is lost. One appears to common people as unbearably proud and boastful. It seems difficult [for such practice to produce] anything but persons whose pure view and disengagement from worldly concerns gradually diminish.

Even the special, outstanding individuals who are the leaders of the spiritual traditions are, in their own way, somewhat similar to [the meditators described above]. They only concern themselves with the study, meditation, teaching, and furthering of their own traditions, without seeking education in any others. Even if they attempt to learn a little about another tradition, they never assist the continuation of its enlightened activity. Those who are involved in spreading their own traditions experience success like a ripening harvest of grain, but in the meantime some very high lineages of meditation practice are close to disappearing into the void.

[On the other hand,] the precious lineage of meditation practice of the Oral Instruction Lineage of the Karmapas in

---

contemplation of the great fortune one has to have been born a free and fully endowed human being, of impermanence and the inevitability of death, of the effects of one's acts, and of the disadvantages of life lived within the bounds of what is called "cyclic existence," the Buddhist vision of the universe as a cosmic rat race.

this region is an integral blend of the streams of two lineages — that from Gampopa and that of the Ancient Instruction Lineage. This union was initiated by the accomplished master Karma Pakshi and the omniscient Rangjung Dorjay [the second and third Karmapas]. In particular, the venerable Rangjung Dorjay was blessed by Vimalamitra [in a vision] and then spread the Heart-Essence of the Karmapa, a meditation which is still practiced. As well, treasure texts from the great treasure revealers of our tradition have gradually become part of [this Oral Instruction Lineage]. [These include treasures discovered] by the undeniably great Sang-gyay Lingpa; the king of Dharma, Rinchen Puntsok; Jatson Nyingpo; Chöjay Lingpa; Mingyur Dorjay; Rolpay Dorjay; Dorjay Drakpo; Chok-gyur Daychen Lingpa, and others. Moreover, Karmapa and his spiritual heirs have assumed the guardianship and established the systems of practice for the treasure teachings of most of the great treasure revealers, including those of the king of Dharma, Ratna Lingpa; Shikpo Lingpa; and Taksham Samten Lingpa, to name a few.

In particular, Karma Chakmay, the emanation of [the bodhisattva] Powerful All-Seeing One [Avalokiteshvara; Chen-ray-zee, *spyan ras gzigs dbang phyug*], was exclusively concerned with furthering the advancement of the long-standing tradition uniting the Oral and Ancient Instruction Lineages. In later years, both the fourteenth Karmapa [Tekchok Dorjay] and the omniscient emanation of the bodhisattva Loving-Kindness [Maitreya; Jampa, *byams pa*], Tenpa Nyinjay [also known as Tai Situpa Chökyi Jungnay], through the series of his incarnations, did even more to spread this tradition far and wide. As a result, the common stream of the philosophical view, activity, and meditation of the Oral and Ancient Instruction Lineages continues unbroken [to the present day].

In a similar manner, the incomparable doctor from Dakpo [Gampopa] was originally a follower of the Buddha's Word as Instruction Lineage. Since his time, the essential basis of meditation [within the Oral Instruction Lineage] has been *The Stages of the Path of the Three Types of Individuals* from the Buddha's Word as Instruction Lineage. To give another example, the second Buddha, the venerable Rangjung Dorjay, was the main heir of the transmissions of The Six Branches of Application [from the Vajra Yoga Instruction Lineage], the Pacification of Suffering Instruction Lineage, the Severance Instruction Lineage and others. As a result, the continuity of the special tradition called the Severance Oral Instruction Lineage continues unbroken to the present day. The great Trungpa of Zurmang Monastery,[4] Kunga Namgyal, furthered the advancement of the Pacification of Suffering Instruction Lineage, as did the all-knowing Chökyi Jungnay for the Six Branches of Application of the Vajra Yoga Instruction Lineage. The fourth Karmapa, Dzamling Rolpay Dorjay, made the doctrines from the Shangpa Instruction Lineage the heart of his meditation and his teaching. Since his day, the series of omniscient Karmapas have consistently upheld and protected the Oral Instruction Lineage of Dakpo (Gampopa) and the Shangpa Instruction Lineage together. The Intensive Practice of the Three Vajras Instruction Lineage is itself a separate transmission of the great accomplished one, Orgyenpa, a member of the golden rosary [of lineage holders] of our tradition.

[The former holders of the Oral Instruction Lineage of the Karmapas] including the lord of Dharma, the venerable Rangjung Dorjay (the third Karmapa); the seventh Karmapa (Chödrak Gyatso); the realized Kachö Wangpo (the second Shamarpa); Sokon Rikpa Raldri; Goshri Paljor Döndrup (the first Gyaltsab Rinpochay); Karma Trinlaypa; the great, glorious Chökyi Döndrup (the eighth Shamarpa); the omniscient Chökyi Jungnay (the eighth Tai Situpa) and others studied and contemplated whatever spiritual instructions could be found in Tibet. Moreover, while each served as the chief of our Oral Instruction Lineage [during his own time], he impartially spread these traditions of explanation and meditation practice. In this way, they were of unsurpassed benefit to the teachings of the Buddha.

How can ordinary persons like us, who can't grasp even a portion of the spiritual path, manage to perpetuate the example of such lives of freedom? Now that I must follow in their footsteps, my sincere wish to respectfully learn from their acts has not diminished. Through the innate strength of this genuine attitude, I never felt I had consumed enough of the nectar of spiritual instructions; I never had enough

---

[4] Zurmang (*zur mang*, "Many-Cornered") is a monastic institution in Eastern Tibet. The incarnation lineage of the founder of that institution, the Trungpa Rinpochays, are specialists in the practices of Severance and the Pacification of Suffering.

confidence to judge as right or wrong, good or bad, that which I considered to be all equally the Buddha's teachings; and I never bound myself in the tight fetters of self-serving competitiveness. Therefore, though I'm now at the end of my life, I still search impartially for spiritual instructions. The virtuous force of this higher motivation which is strengthened by the armor of my enthusiasm, and the powerful force of the small amount of positive actions of many previous lifetimes have had their effects. Specifically, the faultless power of the enlightened vision of the spiritual masters and the Three Jewels has ensured that my wishes have been entirely granted through the pervasive great compassion of my illustrious masters, second Buddha Vajra Holders. [They have granted my wishes by bestowing] the profound and extensive instructions of the paths belonging to the eight great practice lineages of the Himalayan region. These systems of meditation are all untainted by the influence of broken tantric commitments, are unobscured by deceitful lies, and are undiminished in their ability to inspire experience and realization. These lineages of meditative experience continue unbroken and the intensity of their blessing has not become dissipated.

I have become someone in whom rests some tiny fraction of the stream of the instructions which ripen and liberate, but I have not been honored by the pleasing-sounding names of "accomplished one" or "realized one," nor have I become an expert or an authority on the practices of any one lineage of spiritual instruction. However, now that all the minds of the past great masters have passed completely into the realm of totality, I hope to be of some small benefit to the continuity of the teachings and a good example for the next generation of fortunate and intelligent masters. My own good fortune is extremely limited so I may be unable to help anyone at all, but, as the omniscient Dolpopa stated:

> Though you're not able to carry
> Loads weighty or burdensome,
> At least feel concerned
> Toward the decline of Buddhism!

I have not apathetically abandoned the inner heart of the Buddha's teaching and [I hope that] my intention [to help others] will not be unproductive. Therefore, I have created a positive connection to the profound tantric creation and completion phase meditations for the residents of the two retreat centers (of Palpung[5]) by introducing them to the general styles of all eight lineages of meditation practice, except that of the Path and Result Instruction Lineage. The profound instructions of this particular tradition are difficult to teach and practice properly with so much else on the program. But because one half of the Himalayan region is filled with upholders of its tradition, I feel reassured that it can be absent from the programs of the retreats.

For some time now the program of the large retreat center has focused on the profound and extensive creation and completion phase meditations of the Oral Instruction Lineage of Master Marpa, and the practice of Severance. I have established the custom of supplementing this program with the ripening and liberating practices of the Pacification of Suffering Instruction Lineage. Here in this retreat center, we maintain the traditions of the entire cycle of meditations from the Shangpa Instruction Lineage; the Six Branches of Application of the Vajra Yoga Instruction Lineage [supplemented by instruction in] the Intensive Practice of the Three Vajras Instruction Lineage; and the inner heart of the Ancient Instruction Lineage, Great Perfection [Dzok Chen, *rdzogs chen*], along with its inner secret, the Heart Essence practices. In both retreat centers, [the manual called] *The Stages of the Path of the Three Types of Individuals* forms the basis for the preliminary practices. [Between these two centers, then,] seven [of the eight] systems [of meditation practice] are fully represented. (*Catalogue*, pages 94b-97b)

KONGTRUL'S LIFE AND THE NON-SECTARIAN VIEW

Kongtrul is known as one of the foremost masters of the non-sectarian view; however he makes it clear in his autobiography that he did not arrive at this perspective without first experiencing a regrettable bout of sectarianism.

---

[5] Palpung (*dpal spungs*, "Mound of Glory") Monastery, the main seat of the Tai Situpa incarnation lineage, was founded in the late eighteenth century by the eighth Tai Situpa, Chökyi Jungnay. There was a three-year retreat center there; Kongtrul calls it the large retreat center. Kongtrul's own retreat center was located at a short distance from it. Palpung is situated near the city of Dergay in the region called Kham, now part of northwest Sichuan Province, China. It continues to function as a monastic institution.

Kongtrul was born into a non-Buddhist family: his parents were followers of the Bön religion. Although Kongtrul felt a strong affinity to Buddhist masters at a young age to the point of being teased by his Bönpo playmates as "a Buddhist monk," his early training was within the Bön tradition. This was the first but not the last time that Kongtrul allowed his own feelings to be overruled by those around him who were more assertive (his step-father in this case). As he remarks:

> Around this time [about the age of ten], I felt great admiration for anyone who was said to have recognized the nature of mind. Like a thirsty person craving water, I yearned to meet a master who could give me instruction concerning the mind, but I was young and weak. My parents wouldn't help me [find a teacher] so I abandoned the idea.
>
> In general my father was extremely strict. When I was studying reading and writing, attending a ritual, or on other occasions, he would beat me severely if I acted even a little childishly, so it was impossible to do anything except to behave myself. I could not even go outside without first asking his permission. He would relate many examples of other persons who fought, ate and drank to excess, stole, lied, etc., and eventually were excluded from society and he would tell us, "You young people will become like them!" He was always authoritarian and at the time I was anguished, sad, and depressed. Reflecting back [on my childhood], I think my entrance into human society has been due to the kindness of that man, my venerable father. He was exceedingly kind to me and I think it must be hard to find such an honest and conscientious person these days. (*Autobiography*, pages 9b-10a)

Kongtrul explains his own agreeable but pliant nature in this way:

> From an early age I've been of a shy and gentle nature. No matter who might have asked me to do something, I've been attentive to his or her wishes whether I've been capable of doing what was asked or not. Consequently, everyone of any social standing has appreciated and treated me with kindness. (*ibid*, page 12b)

Kongtrul's strict and overbearing father was imprisoned for his involvement in a local dispute when Kongtrul was in his mid-teens. He left home with his mother's encouragement and was eventually hired as a secretary by a Buddhist monk who became his mentor and perhaps a father-figure. Through him Kongtrul soon met a lama from a Buddhist monastery:

> A lama from Shaychen (a Nyingma monastery), Jikmay Losal, arrived and asked me to relate stories of the Bön religion. I spoke for a long time, recounting what I'd heard of Bön. The lama said I had a clear mind and was articulate. [My mentor] remarked that I was bright and that he thought I should engage in the study of Buddhist arts and sciences. He asked the lama what would be best [for my future] and it was thus decided that I should stay with Öntrul Rinpochay of Shaychen Monastery. (*ibid*, page 13a)

This meeting marked Kongtrul's entrance into Buddhism. At the age of sixteen, he accompanied the lama to the monastery and entered it in 1829. His life there might have continued happily but for his mentor who was quite ambitious for Kongtrul and insisted that he leave Shaychen for Palpung, a Kagyu monastic institution. This move in 1833 at the age of twenty soon led to Kongtrul's first negative experience of religious institutions, as he was coerced into re-taking his monastic ordination:

> [My mentor told me that] when our refuge and protector [Tai Situpa, Payma Nyinjay Wangpo] arrived, it was very important that I request full monastic ordination. Along with this advice, he gave me all the requisite articles of a monk. I explained to him how I'd already received the vows at Shaychen. He scolded me with harsh words and said that I must receive monk vows from the victorious one and his spiritual heirs [a reference to Karmapa and the main reincarnate masters of that tradition]. (*ibid*, page 18a)

When the subject was raised again, Kongtrul tried once more to influence the situation, with predictable results:

> [My mentor again] told me that I must take full monastic ordination. I recounted the manner in which I had received those vows in Shaychen [Monastery] from Öntrul Rinpochay and that lama's instructions to me, however he replied, "You absolutely must take vows here. It will be sufficient if [Öntrul] hears that you've given your old vows back." So I never formally offered my vows back. Later, because they give some importance here to spiritual companions, I had no choice but to enter the row [of prospective monks] when there was some important reincarnate lama to take vows with... At the time [of taking the ordination], my mind was so preoccupied with thoughts of my previous vows that I

> never felt that I truly received [the new ones]. (*ibid*, pages 18b-19a)

The worst was yet to come: in order that he might remain at the monastery, Kongtrul was "recognized" as a reincarnation of a past master of that institution. According to Dr. Gene Smith, in his excellent introduction to the Tibetan edition of Kongtrul's *Encyclopedia of Buddhism*, a monastery could be asked to send any of its promising monks at any time to serve in another monastic or political institution higher up the heirarchical ladder. An exception was made in the case of incarnate masters of the monastery, who were exempt from such conscription. Palpung used that loophole to protect Kongtrul against bureaucratic head-hunters from Dergay, the administrative capital of the district. These political maneuvers were instigated by Kongtrul's mentor:

> He had very strong affection for me and great hopes for my career. Because he was afraid that I would be lost to another [institution], he told the lord of refuge [Tai Situpa] that since I might [be called to leave the monastery] suddenly due to unpreventable circumstances, like being summoned as a secretary for the Dergay [administration], it was essential that I be given the name of one of our [monastery's] reincarnate masters. As this was deemed appropriate, I was to be given the name of a reincarnate lama who had been the student of the last [Tai Situpa]. However, Pawo Tsuklak Gawa and Kardruk Rinpochay objected strenuously, arguing that if I were given the names of any of three [former masters] — Alo Kunkyen, Tsewang Kunkyab, or Tamdrin Gonpo — and if I were claimed by the monastery [on that basis], this would be wrong regardless of the justification and would cause great problems later. In spite [of this protest],... it was decided that if I were given the name of the incarnation of a servant and student of the last [Tai Situpa] during the early part of his life, Kongpo Vamteng Trulku, it would form an auspicious connection [to this master]. It was announced locally that I was [this incarnation] so henceforth I was called "Kongtrul" [the first and second-to-last syllables of the name]. (*ibid*, pages 19a-b)

Such procedures must have been a rude and disheartening awakening for Kongtrul. Although he became known as "Kongtrul," he never once used that name when signing any of his works. Within his retreat manual he refers to himself as "Jamgon Lama," and signs it using one of the four different names he habitually used for identifying himself as an author. "Kongtrul" was not one of them.

The shy and gentle monk soon found his attitudes shaped by the sectarian biases prevalent in his new monastic home. He gives a brief picture of this in his autobiography. The year was 1836; he was twenty-three years old:

> Once I walked to the summit of a mountain, then realized that I was dreaming. [Continuing to dream,] I wished to go to [the pure land of Guru Rinpochay,] Tail-Fan Island, and then flew through the air. Behind many mountains circled like the iron mountains [at the edge of the world,] I saw a purple jewel-like mountain that was only half-visible. Its neck was partly visible but its peak was covered by clouds. I thought I should pray as I continued to approach. At that moment, I felt as if a tremendous amount of water was pouring down behind me and I forgot that I was dreaming. I panicked and awoke.
>
> At that time my devotion to the Ancient Instruction Lineage had slightly relaxed and diminished because I felt, "I'm of the Oral Instruction Lineage." I was certain that my karmic obscurations were due to this and I later did confession of [this fault] out of regret. (*ibid*, page 23b)

In another book Kongtrul gives a longer and more detailed account of his spiritual and physical sickness that he attributed to sectarian bias and the gradual healing of his relationship with the treasure texts. The story culminates with his formal recognition as a revealer of concealed treasure texts:

> At fifteen years of age, I met Guru Rinpochay in a dream and received his blessing. Subsequently, I thought of writing many books, including practice texts. In particular, while I was living in Shaychen Monastery, I wrote ceremonies for the propitiation of Glorious Goddess [Lhamo Palchenmo, *lha mo dpal chen mo*] and other texts.... After finishing them, I wrote a practice text for Vajra Hammer [Dorjay Bay-chon, *rdo rje be con*]... [and other texts concerning demons and protectors]. I showed these to Öntrul Rinpochay.[6] The scope of his sacred view was most expansive: he praised my work. He requested the reading transmission for it, practiced the texts for a short time and saw clear signs of their positive effect. He commented that the Glorious Goddess propitia-

[6] There were two Öntrul Rinpochays in Kongtrul's life. This is the last mention of the first, a master from Shaychen Monastery. All later mentions of Öntrul Rinpochay refer to a master resident at Palpung Monastery.

tion would help relieve the present-day sicknesses of people as well as of their livestock, while the Vajra Hammer practice was very effective for relieving the obscuring effect of broken tantric commitments during this degenerate time.

During this period of my life, I strove to further my study and to be diligent in my training to the exclusion of all else. As meditation practice was the most important aspect of this training, all my time was spent with things central to it. I saw very clearly a place of concealment of treasure texts in that area; however I did nothing about it.

Later I went to Palpung Monastery where I received monastic ordination. Once I had passed through the door to the spiritual instructions of the precious Oral Instruction Lineage, I came to accept the advice of its masters and my spiritual companions as valid above all else. As a result, my partiality and attachment to the Later Translation School greatly increased and I experienced something like revulsion toward visionary treasure texts and the like. Moreover, some high lamas who saw the texts I had written previously were openly critical of them. I then burned all my books and wrote a short text of aspiration and vows.

These events caused my dreams and appearing signs to become increasingly disturbed and I was seized by an extremely serious fever not among the thirty varieties then known.[7] Every day I thought I was going to die. One night during that time I had an experience which was impossible for me to ascertain as either dream or reality: I died and met Guru Rinpochay with his consort. After I received answers to some questions, they gave me a firm command to take birth again and I found myself appearing in my bed. As a result, for a few days afterward there were moments when I was convinced that I was in the period between death and rebirth.

I sold the full extent of the few possessions I owned and made representations of the body, speech, and mind [of the Buddha]. Principal among these were thirteen paintings of [the visualization for] the Quintessential Vision of the Spiritual Master [meditations that come from the treasure texts]. This made my health gradually improve. I then went into retreat to practice meditation. Although I was physically weak from being assailed by a disease of the inner energy

---

7 *Bro nad* is written in the text; this seems to be a misprint for *dro nad*, fever.

winds, my experiences and dreams were positive.

At the point when [my health] was most disturbed, the noble precious master [Jamyang Kyentsay Wangpo] remarked [in a letter?] from Dzongsar that the [previously written] propitiation of Glorious Goddess seemed critical for [my recovery]. Furthermore, in a dream, my faithful student Karma Nyi Ö told me that it would be difficult for me to recover without performing the propitiation of the goddess I had written. That propitiation text, however, was gone forever. A text called *An Offering to the Kind Goddess* came to my mind. On the day I wrote it, the positive auspicious sign of a circular tent-like rainbow appeared brilliantly in the deep blue sky. After I had recited the offering a few times, my health gradually improved.

Later the treasure revealer Kundrol Sangwa Tsal (generally called Tsewang Drakpa) arrived in the vicinity. Since we were from the same homeland, I wondered whether I should go to meet him. I requested Jamyang Kyentsay Wangpo for a divination to help me decide. He replied, "This treasure revealer is genuine but due to his excessive wildness, he is just of a middling quality. In spite of that, if you meet him, this will heal your previously damaged connection [to the treasure texts]." I wasn't able to meet him [at that time], however.

My thirty-seventh year was a passage particularly full of obstacles and I contracted several diseases. I did many intensive practices. During the time I was doing the intensive practice of the Quintessential Vision of the Spiritual Master, I dreamed I met Guru Rinpochay. With great respect, I bowed and asked for his blessing which he bestowed with some mantras and words. Then he said, "I will clear away the obstacles to your life this year. In a few years from now you will meet me in real life and at that time you can gradually learn what you need to know." Later, at the age of forty, when I met the great treasure [revealer] Chok-gyur Daychen Lingpa for the first time, I felt like a child being reunited with his father.[8]

From that time forth, this renowned and indisputably

---

[8] The context of this statement and Kongtrul's natural humility make me believe he felt himself to be the child in this case, and Chokling the father. An observer of this encounter between a forty-year-old (Kongtrul) and a young man of twenty-four (Chokling) might have easily assumed otherwise.

genuine treasure revealer gave me guidance in many ways based on treasure texts [that he retrieved both] before and subsequent to our meeting. Although I had just begun the work of compiling *The Treasury of Rediscovered Teachings*, there was justifiable cause at the time for concern about obstacles to my life. He foretold that if vajra feasts for as large a gathering as possible were offered without delay..., my life would reach its limits. This I did unhesitatingly.

Particularly, at the time when the sacred ground at Dzong Shö was unveiled, the omniscient Jamyang Kyentsay Wangpo, the great treasure revealer Chok-gyur Daychen Lingpa, I and others performed the great practice of the Eight Configurations of Deities. In Chitta Sang Puk ["Secret Heart Cave"], immediately after we had finished our practice, the two treasure revealers fashioned a high throne of stone and covered it with a cushion. They offered me the representations of the body, speech, and mind [of the Buddha] as well as the symbolic offering of the universe in the form of the primordial jewel. Then they gave me a name bestowed by Guru Rinpochay, Orgyen Chimay Tennyi Yungdrung Lingpa ["Deathless Seal of Stability of the Two Doctrines"]. They insisted that I should use the name from then on and repair my damaged relationship with the profound treasure texts. They then performed a ceremony to increase my longevity. (*Nectar Appearing in a Mirage*, pages 32b-34b)

This account relates Kongtrul's betrayal of his own feelings and his gradual return to the roots of his personal spiritual life. He learned through difficult experiences to continually broaden his horizons without rejection of what had been important to him in the past. This story is not a tale of Kongtrul abandoning the Oral Instruction Lineage for another. He usually wrote of himself as a member of that lineage and always considered his principal spiritual master to be Tai Situpa, Payma Nyinjay Wangpo, the head of Palpung Monastery and an incarnate master of the Kagyu Lineage of the Karmapas.

The most serious effect of sectarian bias, according to Kongtrul, was that it constituted the highly negative act of the rejection of the Buddha's teaching. Although every Buddhist must decide what methods of spiritual development are personally meaningful among the ocean of teachings given by the Buddha, rejection or disparagement of other Buddhists' very different personal choices from among the same teachings is tantamount to rejection of the Buddha's word. Kongtrul was freed from the last vestiges of his sectarian bias at the age of forty (in 1853) as a result of his contact with Jamyang Kyentsay

Wangpo, an incarnate master of the Sakya monastic system, whose expansive non-sectarian vision had a profound influence on Kongtrul. After providing a long list of the empowerments he had received from Kyentsay at that time, he makes the following comment:

> These days, lamas, scholars, and well-known monks [have appreciation] for only their own tradition of practice and a few of the basic Buddhist source texts. Their sacred view toward the entirety of the Buddha's doctrine is limited and their outlook is very narrow-minded. Those of every rank are generally lacking in knowledge and experience in the teachings of the Buddha.
>
> Lately in particular, those who lack honesty and a pure view toward Buddhism act as if they had some authority. They make numerous statements concerning the quality of spiritual traditions and the purity of lineages. Moreover, apart from [having no interest] in other instruction lineages, they unjustifiably have very strong resistance or avoidance [of practice] in even their own tradition. They are as full of suspicion as a blind yak that runs from its own imagined fears.
>
> As for myself, I sincerely wished [to practice] the instructions for spiritual development; however since I never acquired the mental strength that comes from firm commitment, my will was weak and I didn't accomplish my wishes. From this time forth, however, the flower of impartial faith toward all the teachings and masters of the Buddha's doctrine gradually blossomed within me in all directions. Moreover, my experience in the practice of the teachings became increasingly better. The fact that I have thus avoided committing the extremely serious act of rejecting the Buddha's teaching is due to the kindness of this precious master. (*Autobiography*, pages 66b-67a)

THE EVOLUTION OF KONGTRUL'S RETREAT CENTER

Kongtrul did not initially intend to become the founder of a retreat center; he simply wanted to practice meditation. He first entered a long retreat at the age of twenty-two: he began the three-year, three-fortnight retreat of Palpung Monastery during the tenth lunar month of 1835. He was unable to stay for the entire duration of the retreat, however:

> [In late 1836,] Karmapa [the fourteenth, Tekchok Dorjay] arrived in the area and sent a letter to the lord of refuge [Tai Situpa], asking that I be sent to instruct him in [Sanskrit] grammar. Tai Situpa said that it was impossible for me not to go so I left the retreat. (*ibid*, pages 25b-26a)

Before Kongtrul left for Karmapa's residence, Tai Situpa gave him a number of instructions including one that Kongtrul later realized foretold his becoming the major lineage holder of the Oral Instruction Lineage of the Karmapas:

> He explained that this [single instruction] contained the essence of the meaning of the hundreds and thousands of instructions spoken by Guru Rinpochay concerning the nature of the mind. In the past the noble [eighth Tai Situpa] Chökyi Jungnay had bestowed it upon the powerful victor, Düdul Dorjay, as an instruction pointing out the nature of mind, and then entrusted his lineage to him. This master, the noble thirteenth Karmapa, in turn bestowed this pointing-out instruction and then entrusted the lineage to him [the ninth Tai Situpa, Payma Nyinjay Wangpo]. It seems there was a reason [he gave me this instruction]. (*ibid*, page 26a)

Six years later at the age of twenty-nine, Kongtrul finally decided to leave the monastery to take up solitary residence in an abandoned retreat place. Although he does not relate the death of his mentor at the beginning of that year (1842) to his decision to leave Palpung, there would seem to be some correlation. All he needed now to be able to enter retreat was permission from his master, Payma Nyinjay Wangpo:

> I asked the lord of refuge for permission to live in the retreat place [of the previous Tai Situpa] and sometimes remain in retreat there. At first it seemed difficult that he would agree; finally he promised that I could stay there for three years.
>
> I then disposed of whatever large or small possessions I owned, exchanging them for the material needed to make representations of enlightened form — eleven large fine paintings of the Quintessential Vision of the Spiritual Master, including the guardians of that teaching; representations of enlightened speech — one volume of *The Perfection of Wisdom in Eight Thousand Lines* written in gold; and representations of enlightened mind — one hundred thousand *tsa-tsas* [small models of stupas].
>
> It seems that during the time of Chökyi Jungnay a retreat

> center and monastic practice residence existed at the place of my hermitage. Later, however, the site became ownerless and abandoned after Öntrul Wanggi Dorjay founded the lower retreat center [at Palpung]. Now nothing was left except some decrepit buildings, so one day at the end of autumn I went to investigate and to make fragrant smoke offerings to the gods. At that time there was no distinct path leading to the place but when I arrived behind the [lower] retreat center, a vulture there took flight and I followed in its direction.... It turned to the east and soared away: I looked over in that direction and saw the place of the retreat. When I reached it, I performed the fragrant smoke offering; good signs and portents for the future appeared. Later two monks from another area who appreciated what I was doing assisted me in constructing the semblance of a small house in the ruins of what had been the home of the head lamas. (*ibid*, pages 41a-b)

Kongtrul's final preparation for retreat was to request from his master the empowerment for the meditation he was going to do. At the same time his hermitage was given the name by which it would become known:

> I had received the empowerment of the Gathering of the Jewels many times but I wanted to receive the particular lineage [of the Tai Situpas] so I requested [and received] the empowerment from the precious lord of refuge. [At that time] he gave the name "The Ever-Excellent Abode of Radiant Great Bliss" [Kunzang Daychen Ösel Ling] to the hermitage. When I went to the hermitage I owned nothing but my tattered clothes, a quarter measure of tea, and five measures of barley and yogurt; however, on the fifteenth day of the month the Buddha descended from the heavens [after teaching his mother there, i.e., the ninth lunar month of 1842], I began my retreat. (*ibid*, page 44a)

This time Kongtrul was able to remain in retreat and to live independently. He finished three years in retreat as planned but didn't move back to the monastery after that time: the little hermitage he had built became his home. Twenty years later, he looked back:

> Once I had received the empowerment and reading transmission from the lord of refuge I first spent three years meditating on the entire range of preliminary and main practices of the Gathering of the Jewels. Following this, I performed various practices from the New and Old

Treasures of the Ancient Instruction Lineage, such as the Quintessential Secret [meditation on the spiritual master], the Quintessential Vision of the Spiritual Master, and the Gathering of the Joyful Ones of the Eight Great Configurations of Deities; and practices from the lower and higher tantras of the Later Translations, such as Wheel of Supreme Bliss [Chakrasamvara], Adamantine Joy [Hevajra], and Ocean of Victors [Gyalwa Gyatso, *rgyal ba rgya mtsho*]. I performed the intensive practice of each of these, along with the corresponding completion phase meditations. In particular, while resting in the nature of mind, the heart of Great Seal [Mahamudra] meditation, I borrowed [from the works of others] to compose whatever treatises were appropriate.[9]

It has now been twenty-one years since I moved here. During this time, whatever harmful sicknesses I have experienced due to the arising of the effects of my past negative acts or to the obscuring effect of contact with those who have broken their tantric commitments, etc., have been completely healed through the compassion of the spiritual master and the Three Jewels. Apart from [sickness], no misfortunes whatsoever have occurred; on the contrary, the positive side of my practice has increased.

In particular, I've felt devotion toward Guru Rinpochay since my childhood and faith toward those practices which contain the essence of the million meditations [he taught]. My diligent practice of these has produced believable and visible signs of success: the omniscient Dorjay Ziji Tsal [Jamyang Kyentsay Wangpo], who is Vimalamitra appearing in the form of a spiritual friend, and Orgyen Chok-gyur Daychen Lingpa, the representative of the great master from Oddiyana, his emanated messenger of peace to the world, have both come to this place often, in the past and recently, to open the secret treasury of an ocean of tantric teachings. They have given me many consecrated substances and very sacred objects such as statues, yellow parchment [of the treasure texts], etc. and they have created a boundless number of positive auspicious connections. (*Catalogue*, pages 11a-b)

---

[9] Plagiarism was and is rife in Tibetan scholarship, where it seems to be looked upon favorably as indicative of an author's respect for past masters. This comment by Kongtrul was probably written in a spirit of humility rather than as an admission of wrong-doing.

From his account, it would seem that Kongtrul took up residence in the abandoned retreat center because it had been founded by Chökyi Jungnay, one of the masters who inspired him. As time went on he began to suspect and to receive indications from others that the place was more significant than he had imagined.

Throughout India and the Himalayan region there are areas of sacred ground, places consecrated for meditation by great masters of the past. Some of these are well known: the places blessed by Guru Rinpochay and the places where Milarepa meditated, for example. Others were consecrated by Guru Rinpochay and left concealed as a treasure to be revealed when the area would become of significant benefit to the world. Kongtrul found himself in such a place: it was fully accessible and visible to everyone but no one was aware that this piece of land had any special significance. It was Kyentsay who first confirmed Kongtrul's intuition concerning his area of residence and Chokling who unveiled it formally as sacred ground:

> [In 1856, Kyentsay] declared that this excellent place is the third Devikotri, an external expression of the eye of wisdom at the highest extremity of the central channel. I wondered about that statement since that name for this place was unknown. Later I asked him why he had said it. He replied that at that time he had had a clear meditative experience of hearing it in a secret song of the wisdom dakinis.[10] (*Autobiography*, page 82a)

Devikotri means "The Goddesses' Palace"; the first Devikotri is in India, the second in central Tibet. Both are renowned as areas of sacred ground.

Kyentsay's remark provoked Kongtrul later that year to ask Chokling to describe the special features of the area of his residence. It was subsequent to this that Chokling began calling the area Tsadra Rinchen Drak, now its most commonly used name. *Tsa* is a Tibetan mispronunciation of the first syllable of the Sanskrit word *Charitra* ("Four Refuges"),[11] the name of one of the most important areas of sacred ground in southeast Central Tibet. *Dra* (Tibetan) means "similar to" or "like." Thus the name *Tsadra* indicates that the area of Kongtrul's retreat was equivalent to Charitra in spiritual influence.

[10] In this text, *dakini* (Sanskrit) refers to an enlightened woman, either a human being who has attained supreme accomplishment or a goddess from a buddha's pure realm.

[11] The translation of *Charitra* as "Four Refuges" is according to Kunkyen Payma Karpo in his *Guide Book of Holy Place Charitra* (Darjeeling: Lama Sherab Gyatso, 1982).

Rinchen Drak means "jewel cliff." Of the twenty-five areas of sacred ground in eastern Tibet, it represents the heart of the qualities of enlightenment.

Kongtrul describes the stages of the unveiling of the sacred ground by Chokling and the events that led him to change his life from that of a solitary meditator and author in a tiny hermitage to a builder and master of a meditation center:

> I asked [Chokling] to compose a guide to the sacred features in the area of my home. He replied that the area was one of the twenty-five sacred areas of the Do-Kham region: it was therefore unnecessary to write such a guide as it would have already been concealed as a treasure [long ago]. (*ibid*, page 85b)

In 1857 when Kongtrul was forty-four, Chokling's first attempt to formally unveil the area ended in failure:

> He began walking, intending to introduce us to the features of the heart of the sacred ground; however the protector of the area, Mantra Protectress [Ekajati], appeared clearly before him. To others he appeared to have fainted. (*Guide to the Sacred Ground of Tsadra Rinchen Drak*, page 15a)

In another account of the same incident, Kongtrul relates that Chokling "fainted again and again" due to overpowering visions of Mantra Protectress.[12] Kongtrul continues his account:

> In my dreams and in my discursive thoughts I had wondered whether this place was an area of sacred ground. As well, when I was performing the offering ceremonies for the practices of the original and later tantras, such as the Quintessential Vision of the Spiritual Master, I wondered if a small temple should be built here since the usable space in my house was too small. However I knew that whatever construction was done now would be wasted after my period of residence here. I therefore accepted the discipline of simplicity.
>
> One time later, our refuge and protector, Buddha Vajra Holder [Tai Situpa] said, "The former noble [Tai Situpa]

[12] In the collection of paintings of the masters of the Oral Instruction Lineage, the painting of Kongtrul shows Kyentsay and Chokling seated in front of Kongtrul. The Buddha Vajrasattva soars in space above the three, next to the artists' conception of the main temple and surrounding buildings at Tsadra Rinchen Drak. This protector, Mantra Protectress, is depicted below Kongtrul's throne.

was intently concerned about this retreat place but it has since deteriorated. Now it would be very good if it were restored by [the construction of] a temple and a retreat center. This project must be vigorously undertaken!" In spite of this command, I did nothing specific to fulfill it because, among other reasons, the master was close to passing away.[13]

In 1859 [when the new incarnation of Tai Situpa, Payma Kunzang, appeared].... I vowed that no matter what else I did, I would be sure to construct a small temple at this place. The master, the great treasure revealer [Chok-gyur Daychen Lingpa], arrived at that time.... His vajra words were, "If a temple and retreat center are built at each of the twenty-five great areas of sacred ground in Do-Kham [eastern Tibet], this will pacify all troubles, especially border wars, in the Himalayan region in general, in Do-Kham in particular, and specifically within the respective districts. These [areas of sacred ground] are locations[14] of this pacifying power. A person to construct these buildings will appear in connection with each area of sacred ground. In this place, it's you. To begin with, it's essential that you make a statue of glorious Yangdak Heruka. The material for the form and the objects to put within it [for its consecration] are probably [concealed as] treasures in this vicinity." Although I had no wealth with which to make great buildings, I appreciated the special circumstances and promised to do exactly as he commanded.

Together with Öntrul Rinpochay [of Palpung], I again requested [Chokling] to unveil the treasure of this sacred ground. We received the following letter in reply, affixed with his personal seal:

> In answer to your request that the area of sacred ground at Palpung, Tsadra Rinchen Drak, be unveiled, I ask that you do as is explained in *The Prophecy of the Dakinis of the Three Sources*:
>
> > This supreme sacred place, Tsadra, the mind of enlightenment,

[13] Here Kongtrul uses a polite formula to mention the death of his master: "He was approaching the time he decided to help other beings." In other words, to be reborn in other circumstances.

[14] In this case, the word used in Tibetan for "location" (may tsa, *me btsa'*) is the geographical equivalent of an acupuncture point on the body.

Is formed like the eight channel-spokes at the heart.
When the temple of the glorious *heruka*[15] at the eastern gate is begun
And the local guardian's shrine and statue are complete,
Then can the sacred ground be unveiled: take great heed!

and in *The Proclamation of the Prophecies*:

A temple in the Uk Valley[16] built by this emanation
Who passes on to Mi-go Tsek in the east.
Shakya and Lodru, Bero's emanations,
Will build a temple at Tsadra, mound of jewels;
A statue of the glorious heruka
Which liberates through sight, sound, thought or touch;
A retreat for the three inner tantras
Where the diligent will surely gain freedom.

and in *The Secret Transmission of the Dakinis*:

Fire will surely cause the monastery's destruction:
Construct the glorious heruka's temple in the northern direction!

As is said in these texts, a spiritually advanced person will appear at the center of each of the twenty-five areas of sacred ground, the main sacred areas [of this region]. If each of these persons constructs a temple, nothing further need be done to ensure the happiness of Tibet and Kham.

In this case, a temple of the heruka must be constructed on the eastern side of the sacred area, symbolizing the eastern entrance to the channel of

---

[15] *Heruka* (a Sanskrit word) refers in general to wrathful or semi-wrathful tantric deities. Specifically in this context, a statue of Yangdak Heruka, one of the principal deities of the Tantras of the Original Translations, was the main figure within the temple built at Tsadra Rinchen Drak.

[16] This is a reference to Shakya Jungnay (1002-1062), a great master of the Ancient Instruction Lineage who constructed a temple in the Uk Valley. Kongtrul was considered to be an incarnation of this master as well as Berotsana and many others. When I complained to Tsa-tsa Drubgen Rinpochay of Kanding, China, that this verse was difficult to understand, he remarked, "This is a verse of prophecy: prophecies are *supposed* to be obscure!"

> wisdom. The base of the wish-fulfilling tree is the support for Mantra Protectress. In connection to this, a shrine for this protectress should be made at the eastern entrance. Since [these preparations] are important for the actual unveiling of the sacred area, please discuss with the spiritual brothers [of Tai Situpa], and the treasurers and general-secretaries [of the monastic administration] to see if these wouldn't be possible. Please send me a clear reply to this.

He also declared that both the yellow parchment [treasure texts] and the secret prophecies clearly stated that this monastic center [Palpung] was in great danger of being destroyed by fire [or] by enemies. The solution to this was to build a temple dedicated to the great glorious one [Yangdak Heruka] on the northern side [of the hill]. If this were done, no harm would befall [Palpung]. [He warned that] if the auspicious circumstances of this moment were [not seized and if work was] delayed, it would be of no use whatsoever: the temple had to be finished this year!

I hadn't previously collected wood and other materials that could be used for the construction and my livelihood came from begging in the region: I had nothing on hand with which to build a temple. Therefore I asked Öntrul Rinpochay, a pillar of the doctrine of the practice lineage, if the monastic administration would sponsor the construction of the outer temple. If they did so, I would sell whatever objects of value I owned to gradually complete the other buildings and the large and small statues for the interior. He agreed because of his expansive concern for Buddhism. Once he gave his permission by issuing an explanatory directive to the members of the administration, it was decided that the temple would be built.

My thought at the time was that even though the temple itself was completed, if it had no specific owner, it would be difficult for the general owner, the monastic administration, to preserve the place over a long period. Therefore I wondered if it was a good idea to start a small retreat center connected to the temple here. I requested a divination on this subject from the very erudite master, Dabzang Rinpochay. He reported having extremely positive dream signs which indicated that [such a center] would be helpful to Buddhism. I also asked the omniscient master, Dorjay Ziji Tsal [Kyentsay]: he reported that he had had a special vision that portended success. Based on his reassurance, I fully undertook the construction of the retreat houses and surrounding buildings. (*Catalogue*, pages 11b-14a)

In 1859 Chokling tried again to inaugurate the sacred ground and was successful. This event cleared the way for the founding of the three-year retreat center at Tsadra Rinchen Drak.

Kalu Rinpochay related the following account of Kongtrul's original impulse to found a meditation center, here translated by Lama Drubgyu Tenzin of Canada:

> One time, Jamgon Kongtrul the great, already an important lama of Palpung Monastery, had entered a strictly sealed retreat. During the course of this retreat he heard that the principal holder of the Shangpa Instruction Lineage, one Lama Norbu [Shenpen Özer] was to visit Palpung. Kongtrul was already familiar with the Shangpa tradition and had profound respect for these teachings. He had also heard that Lama Norbu was an extraordinary individual. He felt the opportunity to receive the transmission directly from this, the actual lineage holder, was an extremely rare one, and so made the decision to break his retreat in order to meet this person.
>
> Hearing of the arrival of Lama Norbu, Kongtrul left his retreat and made his way to the visitor's apartments to pay his respects, and investigate the possibility of receiving transmission from this lama. Upon arriving in Lama Norbu's room, Kongtrul found he was completely ignored. Although one of the principal lamas of the monastery, it was as though he didn't exist! To Jamgon Kongtrul's great consternation, as long as he remained, no sign was given that he was even present.
>
> Very disturbed by this turn of events, Kongtrul returned to his own rooms. He reflected on his misfortune, and wondered what former negative actions he must have committed to so rupture his connection to the Shangpa tradition and its lineage holder. At no point did he entertain any thought critical of Lama Norbu; rather he examined himself again and again to discern his own faults. So concerned was he that he did not sleep that night but passed the whole of it reflecting on his own shortcomings, performing confession and purification, and reciting the mantra of Vajrasattva.
>
> As dawn was approaching an idea entered into Kongtrul's mind. Perhaps by offering to establish a retreat center expressly dedicated to the propagation of the teachings of the

> Shangpa tradition he would be able to make atonement and so be able to establish a fruitful personal connection with these teachings! The more he considered this idea, the more convinced he became of its appropriateness.
>
> First thing in the morning, then, Kongtrul once again made his way to the rooms of Lama Norbu with this idea foremost in his mind. As he was entering the room, before he could say a word, Lama Norbu addressed him saying, "That is an excellent idea! I don't have the time at the moment to give you all the transmissions, but you should go ahead with this plan and I will return as soon as possible to give you the full transmission of the Shangpa cycle of teachings."

Although this story does not appear in Kongtrul's autobiography, he reports having met this lama for the first time in 1840 (at the age of twenty-seven) and was given just a few instructions on that occasion. He received the full transmission of the Shangpa Instruction Lineage from Lama Norbu in 1843.

THE THREE-YEAR RETREAT AT TSADRA RINCHEN DRAK AND THE REMAINDER OF KONGTRUL'S LIFE

The first three-year, three-fortnight retreat at Tsadra Rinchen Drak began in 1860; Kongtrul was forty-seven years old. Eight persons lived in the small community: a vajra master, five retreatants (of which one was the lama of the protector temple), a cook, and a woodsman. Future retreats during Kongtrul's lifetime involved the same number of participants.

The start of the retreat marked the beginning of a very productive period in Kongtrul's life. He first gave empowerments and instruction at the beginning of the retreat and wrote the retreat manual here translated as *Jamgon Kongtrul's Retreat Manual*. During the following years he spent most of his time in the Palpung area and managed to complete an astounding number of books. It was during this time that Jamyang Kyentsay Wangpo predicted that Kongtrul would complete what Kyentsay called "The Five Treasuries." Kongtrul had already completed *The Treasury of Tantric Instructions of the Oral Instruction Lineage*, a work begun in 1853 and completed in 1855, and he was busy compiling *The Treasury of Rediscovered Teachings*. It was during the period of the first retreat that he composed another of the treasuries, *The Encyclopedia of Buddhism*. This work is noteworthy in this context because Kongtrul made it required reading for prospective retreatants. The year was 1862, Kongtrul was forty-nine years old:

> At that time Lama Ngaydon insisted that I write a treatise on the three disciplines.[17] He promised that if I wrote [the root text], he would compose a commentary to it. However I reflected that treatises on the three disciplines are very common and that in addition to such a treatise, a complete explanation of the Buddhist path would be helpful for those unfamiliar with it. With that thought in mind, I wrote a root text describing the three trainings called *The Encompassment of All Knowledge* in my spare time between meditation sessions.[18] Later I showed it to my noble spiritual master [Jamyang Kyentsay Wangpo] who exclaimed, "This work is really due to the blessings of the spiritual master and to the dakinis opening your inner channels! This must be considered the first of your *Five Treasuries*. You must be sure to write a commentary to this work. It is excellent." (*Autobiography*, pages 100b-101a)

Kongtrul composed the commentary to the text a year later:

> From this time [close to the end of the fourth month of 1863] until the end of the seventh, I was able to write the commentary to [the root text of] *The Encyclopedia of Buddhism* since I had the helpful assistance of the erudite master Tashi Özer as secretary. (*ibid*, page 105a)

This *Encyclopedia of Buddhism* Kongtrul mentions writing in less than four months has two parts: a root text of 160 pages entirely in verse called *The Encompassment of All Knowledge* and a 2,000-page commentary called *The Boundless Ocean of Knowledge*. For most scholars, a work of such breadth and depth might take the better part of a lifetime to complete.

By the end of the first retreat, Kongtrul was advising prospective retreatants to read the treatise before their retreat began:

---

[17] The three disciplines (dompa sum, *sdom pa gsum*) refer to the vows of personal liberation, the commitments of the path of the bodhisattva, and the obligations of tantric practice.

[18] Kongtrul included a lengthy and thorough explanation of the three disciplines in *The Encyclopedia of Buddhism*—Part Five of that work. Despite Kongtrul's treatment of the subject, Lama Ngaydon himself wrote a root text for a treatise of the three disciplines and Tashi Chöpel, one of Kongtrul's main disciples, wrote a commentary to the text. The three trainings are in ethical behavior, meditative absorption, and appreciative discernment.

> Before entering either retreat [i.e., his own and the one at Palpung], the retreatants should study the entire *Encyclopedia of Buddhism*, or if that much study and reflection is not feasible, they should at least have understood the fifth section of the book, which explains the characteristics of master and disciple and how to rely on the master, and [provides complete details of] the three disciplines. (*Catalogue*, page 97b)

Those lines were written in 1864 as the first three-year, three-fortnight period drew to a close. By the end of his life, at least seven and perhaps eight such retreats had been completed in the Ever-Excellent Abode of Radiant Great Bliss. Kongtrul wrote most of his books there and, to judge from the number of texts he said were written for the benefit of the retreatants, he found the retreat a constant source of stimulation for his writing.

In spite of becoming the director of a retreat center and an increasingly important master, Kongtrul adopted none of the style of high lamas. He preferred to live simply without an entourage or attendants, as he remarks in his autobiography when regretting the serious illness of his niece, Rikdzin Drönma, in 1870:

> Since the time I stayed in strict retreat [by myself], I have kept no attendant except when it was absolutely necessary. No monk has stayed here on a regular basis [in that function]. Later, even when the construction work [on the temple and statues] greatly increased, my venerable mother took care of the small needs of the household. Except for her, there has never been someone called treasurer or general secretary here, as is the custom for high lamas or in monastic administrations. If a monk [in that position] was of a higher rank than me, I would find myself overruled by him; if he was of a lower rank, he would resort to stealing or lying, etc., and therefore be unsuitable. Those equal to me are unable to be discreet because of the temper of the times and I've never found anyone who can be a dependable long-time companion. I've not looked for any monk-attendant; after my mother passed away, my niece took her place. (*Autobiography*, pages 119a-b)

1870 must have been a difficult year for Kongtrul: one of his spiritual masters and main sources of inspiration, Chok-gyur Daychen Lingpa, passed away at the age of forty-one. Kongtrul was having to witness the fulfillment of his prediction that he would outlive both Chokling and Kyentsay. They had once competed among themselves in a horse race which Chokling won, with Kyentsay coming in second and Kongtrul last. Kongtrul had started crying at the finish line, which made the spectators remark, "Really! It's only a game!" To which Kongtrul replied, "No! It was an indication of who will reach the Copper-Colored Mountain (the pure land of Guru Rinpochay) first. I'm going to be left here all alone!"

Kongtrul's happiness with his life at Tsadra Rinchen Drak and the retreat, so evident in some of the books he wrote in the early 1860s, eventually faded. This change of heart had nothing to do with the retreat, however. Beginning in 1873, a group of monks from Palpung made vociferous complaints against him and Öntrul Rinpochay, particularly the latter. The new Tai Situpa was probably too young to influence the situation. The state of affairs became so agitated at the monastery that Öntrul Rinpochay passed away suddenly in 1874. Kongtrul was devastated. He explains carefully that he knew that only a few monks were responsible for the tragedy while the rest were entirely free of blame. But the incident itself and the stubborn refusal of the monks to admit their mistake and apologize affected him deeply:

> Their repayment of Öntrul Rinpochay's kindness in such an aberrant manner made me feel revulsion toward all the lamas and monks [there]. For fourteen years after [this tragedy], I never went to the monastery. Even my activity of giving instructions, etc. in [Palpung's] retreat center was curtailed by the strength of my feelings. While I could have moved to any of the large or small monasteries of the Original or Later Schools, I decided to stay here in consideration of the commitments I had taken personally with Payma Nyinjay Wangpo and his spiritual brothers. (*ibid*, pages 133a-b)

Even years later, in 1892, as he contemplates the life and death of one of his young retreatants, Namgyal Dorjay, his sadness over the incident lingers:

> He first came to see me when he was just beginning to talk; he learned how to recite correctly *The Seven-Line Invocation of Guru Rinpochay*. Later he proved to be bright and naturally inclined to virtuous practice. He completed the four hundred thousand accumulations of the preliminary practices for Great Seal meditation and trained in some of the meditation itself. He completed the intensive practices of Ratna Lingpa's Vajra Dagger meditation, as well as that of the Quintessential Secret meditation on Great Compassion. He entered the retreat planning to continue his practice and I had hoped that he would be a person who would be

> of some benefit to himself and others. But due to the negative influence of the broken tantric commitments within this monastery before and the general temper of the time now, all of us, myself included, have succumbed to the power of obstacles, no matter how good we are. This young man, for example, was unable to live for more than twenty-three years. (*ibid*, pages 184b-185a)

1892 was also the year that Kyentsay passed away at the age of seventy-two. Kongtrul, now seventy-nine and still very active, then wrote a superb biography of his master and friend. His own autobiography was completed in 1894 but he continued to compose books even during the last year of his life, 1899, by which time his health would only allow him to give dictation. Even then, at the age of eighty-six, his mind was lucid enough that he composed long and detailed treatises as well as descriptions of complex meditations in verse. Until the end of his life, the heart of his spiritual life and his major concern was meditation. These words were written near the end of his autobiography:

> Concerning my life in general, I first attained this special circumstance — the precious free and bountiful life as a human being, fully endowed with the special characteristics of the seven qualities of higher existences and the four great cycles.[19] I gave my life its real meaning by entering the gate to the precious doctrine of the Buddha. Furthermore, I encountered the Vajra Way of Secret Mantra which has never appeared before, does not appear now and will never appear again.[20] My life has been like a journey to an island of gold and jewels where I could take whatever I chose, a [seemingly] impossible opportunity within this world. However due to the overpowering force of ripening[21] karma

---

[19] The seven qualities of higher existences are a good family, pleasant appearance, a long life, freedom from sickness, good fortune, wealth, and intelligence. The four great cycles are to stay in a harmonious region, to rely on a spiritually advanced person, to formulate positive aspirations, and to cultivate merit.

[20] Vajra Way of Secret Mantra (Sang Ngak Dorjay Tekpa, *gsang sngags rdo rje theg pa*) is the highest of the three systems of spiritual development taught by the Buddha — the Lesser Way, the Great Way, and the Vajra Way. Of all the buddhas, very few are said to teach the Vajra Way. A vajra symbolizes both emptiness and indivisibility; the recitation of mantras forms a central part of many meditations within this system.

[21] The text here has *smon* (aspiration); I believe the word should be *smin*, ripen.

> and to losing my independence to others' control, I am empty-handed of what I wanted — to engage in the heart of meditation practice — and I have been distracted by work I didn't have in mind — endless cycles of activity. (*ibid*, page 189a)

His deep humility, a constant presence in his books, would seem to be genuine, but he follows these words with a full and precise summary of the study, teaching, writing, and meditation he did during his lifetime. It leaves the reader breathless. As one of his closest disciples, Tashi Chöpel, accurately remarks:

> This noble master strove to study every subject. He began with an education in reading and writing within the context of the study of the common arts and sciences, and he continued to pursue a higher education [within Buddhism]. There was nothing he did not learn: from the three collections of the Buddha's teaching to the extraordinary Vajra Way, his studies included even the most minor empowerments, transmissions, meditation instructions, styles of explanation, and practical procedures of the four classes of tantra. The complete record of his education extends to two volumes. An examination of it gives the impression that he spent his entire life studying. The extent of his bestowal of empowerments, reading transmissions, and instructions from the canonical and treasure teachings of the Later and Original Schools gives the impression that he spent his entire life teaching. [This master] was unlike those who finish their study and reflection with a rough understanding [of the subjects]. They then wish to write and compose, and call the few words they write with a competitive spirit and desire for fame "My Collected Works." Unlike these persons, this master's work furthered the continuity of the Buddha's entire doctrine at a time when it was about to expire. The extent of his spiritual instructions, principally contained in the wonderful *Five Treasuries*, fills ninety volumes.[22] When one considers this aspect of his life of freedom, one has the impression that he spent his entire life writing. An examination of how he performed the intensive practices of an ocean of meditations from the discourses and tantras of

[22] The modern edition of *The Five Treasuries*, published under the auspices of Dingo Kyentsay Rinpochay, extends to over a hundred volumes. Moreover, some of Kongtrul's large treatises are not included in this edition.

> the Later and Original Schools gives the impression that his whole life was spent [meditating] within a strictly sealed meditation room. This master's life of freedom[23] can only be understood by awakened persons; [to persons like us] it is inconceivable. This account is not a dishonest exaggeration written [in memory of] my own master; it is an account reflecting the whole truth. Its verity will be clearly evident to the wise. (*The Last Days*, pages 6a-b)

In conclusion, Kongtrul was never interested in becoming a political force through amassing land, buildings, and followers. He made no effort whatsoever to destroy existing institutions or to create new ones, except for his tiny retreat center. His ideas and his writing are a liberation for those who wish to partake freely of all the richness of Buddhist scholastic and meditative traditions. He himself spent his long life practicing and nurturing these in a singular and single-minded abandonment of all else.

KONGTRUL'S RETREAT CENTER AFTER KONGTRUL

As Kongtrul had hoped, his retreat center continued to function after his death. The responsibility of leading the retreat was assumed by others, although it is difficult to find a record of the names of the masters who did so. By 1920, Norbu Döndrup was the retreat master who welcomed into the retreat the young son of Ratok Tulku, an incarnate master who had been a disciple of Kongtrul. Norbu Döndrup recognized that the sixteen-year-old boy, Karma Drubgyu

---

[23] *Life of freedom* (nam tar, *rnam thar*) is a term used to describe the life of a great master or for the recorded story of that life. Kongtrul gives the textbook definition of the term at the beginning of his *nam tar*, i.e., autobiography:

> *Nam tar* in Sanskrit is *vimoksha*, meaning complete freedom or complete liberation. It is the recounting of the story of [the attainment of complete freedom]. In the case of an ordinary person, it is complete freedom from life in the miserable existences attained through pure faith. In the case of an above-average person, it is complete freedom from the ocean of cyclic existence attained through pure disengagement [from worldly concerns]. In the case of an exceptional person, it is complete liberation from the extremes of cyclic existence and perfect peace attained through pure higher motivation [to help others]. In brief, a *nam tar* is the telling of the most excellent story — that of the attainment of complete freedom from suffering and its causes and the subsequent acts which liberate others from their limitations. (page 4a)

Tenzin, was to become the lineage holder of the instructions he had received from Kongtrul and two of that master's main disciples (Tashi Özer and Tashi Chöpel, mentioned above). At the successful conclusion of the retreat, the young man, now known as Lama Kalu (a contraction of his name) went away to pursue further study and later stayed in retreat for twelve years.

Norbu Döndrup continued as master of the retreat until the mid-1940s, when he decided to retire. Lama Kalu was summoned from his retreat to take his master's place, by order of Tai Situpa, Norbu Döndrup, and the sixteenth Karmapa, who was visiting Palpung. According to a member of Palpung's religious community at the time, Lama Tsondru, this choice provoked some consternation among the lamas at Palpung: with so many of them to choose from, why had an outsider been designated as master of the retreat? Karmapa declared that Lama Kalu was in fact an incarnation of Jamgon Kongtrul but that giving him formal recognition would create obstacles to his activity and longevity. However Karmapa informally acknowledged the identity of this lama, who became known as Kalu Rinpochay, in a prayer for his long life in which he wrote, "You continue the life of freedom of Jamgon Lama in the present day."

Kalu Rinpochay lived at the retreat center with Kyentsay Özer, another incarnation of Jamgon Kongtrul. They would often meditate together in a small park above the retreat center where they each planted a pine tree. These trees are still standing today. After the completion of the first retreat under his direction, Kalu Rinpochay decided to reconstruct and enlarge the retreat center. The new center had rooms for twenty-five persons. By the mid-1950s Kalu Rinpochay had left the retreat center for Lhasa and then Bhutan and India. The center fell into disuse and was destroyed during the 1960s.

Following Kalu Rinpochay's design, a new structure was built during the mid-1980s. By mid-1991 one three-year, three-fortnight retreat had been completed at the new center and another was about to begin. The retreat is presently under the direction of an elderly nephew of Norbu Döndrup, Kalu Rinpochay's main spiritual master.

Jamgon Kongtrul's Retreat Manual

Invocation and Resolution

Om Swasti Siddham Shri Jaya Tiktrantu
(The auspicious accomplishments of the venerable victorious ones are presented here.)

I bow to you, my spiritual master, chief of three great mysteries:
Your body's marks and signs whose splendor lights the world and realms of peace;
Your voice of gods, sole source of boundless spiritual instruction;
Your wisdom which embraces space in its deep tranquility.

I set forth to write a guide, a source of comfort and cheer,
Describing rules of discipline for all who practice here—
Those present and future renunciants in the hermitage
At Palpung, the central pillar of the Practice Lineage.

Introduction

During your past lives, you accumulated a great amount of merit and focused it with pure aspirations. The strength [of those aspirations] has now provided you with something more [precious] than a wish-fulfilling jewel: the best [of all possible] lives — your present free and bountiful life [as a human being]. You've been able to encounter the inner heart of the Buddha's teaching, the Vajra Way of Secret Mantra. You have the opportunity of relying on any qualified, lineage-holding spiritual guide you choose. All the favorable conditions for the practice of the instructions for spiritual development are gathered [in your life], and you're able to apply yourself to the heart of that practice. [Your good fortune] — like that of a beggar who dreams he or she owns a wish-fulfilling jewel — might seem impossible but there it is, right in the palm of your hand!

Deep down, though, you might only think of becoming a lama and would feel content just to have stayed the full three-year, three-fortnight period in the retreat center. [In this way,] without purity of intention and conduct, and with a sub-standard level of meditation, you [will only succeed] in cheating the generous persons who provide the wherewithal of your survival [while in retreat], and you will fail to give your life its real meaning. Therefore, it is essential that you prepare a faultless foundation [for your practice].

As a basis, all those who stay here in retreat should have confidence in the three disciplines and have studied and reflected a little upon the Buddha's discourses and tantras during the course of a rainy season retreat.[1] Particularly, admission [to retreat] should be given to those who will practice meditation with [the circumstances of] future lives and the freedom of awakening foremost in their minds. Being careless and unconcerned about this will only result in [others'] material support being wasted and nothing else. Therefore admission should be granted only after careful consideration.

In order to practice [meditation] in retreat, you must first [prepare] a proper foundation by [ensuring] that your intention [to meditate wholeheartedly] is irreversible. During your retreat you should please others by your application to the view, meditation, and conduct of Buddhist practice. Finally, you should satisfy yourself by [ensuring] that the result of your meditation is not wasted. [These are the three] main subjects of the rules of discipline [described below].

---

[1] A rainy season retreat (yar nay, *dbyar gnas*), often a period of study rather than meditation, is held during the Asian monsoon season.

I. Preparation for and Entrance into Retreat

MENTAL PREPARATION FOR THE RETREAT

What is the irreversible intention that is needed? *The Mound of Jewels Discourse* states:

> Kasyapa, if a fully ordained person[2] plans to enter a hermitage [to meditate], he or she should formulate eight resolutions. What are they? He or she should resolve, "I completely renounce this body of mine. I dedicate my life completely [to this effort]. I reject any honors given to me. I renounce all attachment and desire. I will stay in a mountain retreat like a mountain goat [remains in the mountains]. I will train in every aspect of conduct in the hermitage. I will stay there nourished by the instructions for spiritual life. I will not nourish myself with the obscuring emotions." These are the eight resolu-

[2] A fully ordained person (gelong, *dge slong*) has accepted all the vows of a monk or nun.

tions. Fully ordained persons who wish to enter a hermitage should remain there sustained by them.

In brief, you must put all worldly concerns behind you and enter the retreat with the sincere intention to attain unsurpassable great awakening. The lord of spiritual life, Jikten Sumgon, stated:

> How events unfold depends upon [your development of] the mind of awakening, so you must be extremely careful about [your initial attitude toward your retreat]. When going to the mountains to meditate, your intention to reach awakening must not be mingled with other thoughts. If you go to a mountain retreat with disdain for companions or others, you will not accomplish your goals. Like a dog wading into [deep] water, your situation will progressively worsen. If you go to a mountain retreat to gain control of others or with thoughts of [eventually obtaining] food, wealth, or pleasure, you will lose your vows while accumulating [the effects of] the negative acts of others [you have caused] to lose faith. If you go to a mountain retreat in anger, or with similarly negative thoughts, everyone will slander you in hatred. If you go to a mountain retreat with thoughts of pride, good qualities will not arise in your stream of experience. If you go to a mountain retreat thinking of increasing your [stock of] food, clothing, and other [possessions], [not only] will you be without [new] food and clothes, you'll lose those you had. If you go to a mountain retreat thinking only of your own wishes, it won't benefit you or others, since that attitude resembles that of the Way of the Listeners.[3] If you go to a mountain retreat in ignorance, unconscious of the negative effects of

---

[3] The Way of the Listeners (Nyentö Kyi Tegpa, *nyan thos kyi theg pa*) is the most elementary style of Buddhist practice. Although it forms the basis of much of later Buddhist theory and practice, one of the attitudes that characterize this approach to spiritual development is self-centeredness. It is this which the author is criticizing here.

those states of mind, it is said that your practice of virtue will not develop, will be unprofitable, and will lead to negative actions.

How can we prevent those things from happening? he was asked.

He replied, You yourself have the power to do so at this time. This is why I always describe the many benefits of the mind of awakening. If you go to a mountain retreat with thoughts of love, all discord [in your life] will be pacified and events will unfold auspiciously. If you go to a mountain retreat with thoughts of compassion, others will benefit. If you go to a mountain retreat with thoughts of sympathetic joy [in others' happiness], gods, spirits and humans will all think kindly of you. If you go to a mountain retreat with thoughts of equanimity, you will gain control of appearing phenomena. If you go to a mountain retreat with thoughts of all four of these immeasurable attitudes [love, compassion, sympathetic joy, and equanimity], you will succeed in benefitting yourself and others through the four forms of enlightened activity.[4]

If you go to a mountain retreat devoted to the meditation deity, you will attain the ordinary accomplishments. If you go to a mountain retreat devoted to your spiritual master, you will attain supreme accomplishment.[5]

In general, if you go to a mountain retreat with exceptionally good thoughts, you will achieve excep-

---

[4] The four forms of enlightened activity are among the anticipated results of effective meditation within the Vajra Way. They are pacification (of sickness, suffering, and negative influences of all sorts), increase (of well-being, wisdom, and merit), influence (including self-control, as well as over others and events), and forceful action (to confront and overcome obstacles directly).

[5] Ordinary accomplishments (tunmong gi ngödrup, *thun mong gi dngos grub*) are side-effects of meditation. In a general sense, these could include anything as mundane as a calm mind but the term's specific use is confined to eight special powers. Supreme accomplishment (choggi ngödrup, *mchog gi dngos grub*) is the understanding of the nature of one's own mind.

> tional success. If you go to a mountain retreat with moderately good thoughts, you will achieve moderate success. If you go to a mountain retreat with average thoughts, at least your practice of virtue will develop and obstacles won't arise.

Therefore, as is said here, it is crucial that you determine your intention correctly. [Formulating your] initial motivation is like planting a seed. [According to the different kinds of seeds planted,] the individual stalks and grains of wheat, barley, buckwheat, or peas will ripen. Thus, once you have entered retreat in a mountain hermitage, it is extremely important that you never be without the conscious thought that you are there to attain the indivisible state[6] of the Buddha Vajra Holder during this lifetime for the benefit of all beings, your venerable mothers, whose [numbers] fill all of space. It is essential that you never, ever, relinquish that intention by entertaining such misguided thoughts as "I need to receive the title of lama," or "If I receive it, I'll never be without gifts and food," or "I should surpass my spiritual companions," or "I should become as [successful as] other lamas."

PRACTICAL PREPARATION FOR THE RETREAT

Once you have decided to enter retreat on the day of the waxing or waning moon that the retreat is sealed and [to remain inside] until the date it reopens, you must [prepare yourself by] learning [many procedures and skills] well enough so that you are able to perform them without hesitation. These include the order of recitation [of prayers, descriptions of meditations, etc.] for whatever rituals are performed in this retreat center; the way to prepare offerings; the tunes for prayers and ritual music; how to make tormas[7] [of the appropriate styles]; and how to play

---

[6] The indivisible state (zung juk gi gopang, *zung 'jug gi go 'phang*) refers to the accomplishment of both enlightenment itself and its physical manifestations.

[7] Offerings of torma (*gtor ma*) are unique to Himalayan tantric Buddhism. Tormas are traditionally made from a mixture of roasted barley or wheat

the various ritual musical instruments.

The texts that you will need for recitation are the following:

- *The Seven Prayers* [by Guru Rinpochay] with the corresponding description of the meditation [to be done concurrently]
- The various supplications to the [spiritual masters of] the Jonang and Minling[8] [traditions] and those to the [ninth Tai Situpa], Payma Nyinjay Wangpo
- The ceremony for the purification and renewal [of the three disciplines] that cultivates [merit and awareness]
- [The following meditations from the tradition of] Minling: Vajrasattva, Yangdak [Heruka], and all parts of the ritual of the Quintessential Vision of the Spiritual Master (including the activity ritual [called] *The Beautiful Garland of Flowers* and the brief fulfillment ritual for the protectors of the instruction)[9]

---

flour and butter and are decorated with colored butter. Nearly every tantric meditation has a torma of a specific shape and color unique to that practice. Some tormas represent the deity, some are offerings to deities or protectors, and others are dedicated to spirits, demons, or ordinary beings.

[8] Both Jonang (*jo nang*, a place name) and Minling (an abbreviation of Mindrol Ling, *smin grol gling*, "Place of Maturation and Liberation") are names of monastic institutions in central Tibet. Jonang was founded by Tukjay Tsöndru and was the main center for the practice of the Shangpa and Vajra Yoga Instruction Lineages. Mindrol Ling, founded by Gyurmay Dorjay, was a center for the practice of the Ancient Instruction Lineage.

[9] An activity ritual (lay jang, *las byang*) is a text that contains all the stages of a ritual associated with a specific tantric deity.

A fulfillment ritual (kangwa, *bskang ba*) is usually addressed to the protectors of Buddhism. Offerings made in the course of rituals are often those offered to any deity (food, incense, flowers, etc.); fulfillment offerings are those which are personally satisfying to one specific deity. For example, a cup of ordinary tea is given to any visitor to a Tibetan home; a special guest might be given a cup of tea brewed from what the host knows is the guest's favorite kind of tea. The first corresponds to a general offering; the second, to a fulfillment offering.

- The practice texts and the offering ritual[10] for the nine deities [in the configuration] of Wheel of Time
- [The following meditations from] the Shangpa Instruction Lineage: the five deities [in the configuration] of Wheel of Supreme Bliss; [the configuration of] the Five Tantric Deities, condensed to include only the central deities;[11] and White and Red Celestial Women
- The rituals from [both] the Original and Later Schools of Translation[12] for offering the universe in a symbolic form to Tara
- The three practices of the Secret Vital Essence from the New Treasures[13]
- *The Vajrasattva Practice of Liberation Through Hearing* and *The Ritual for the Recitation of* The Heart of the Lotus Tantra

---

[10] An offering ritual (chö chok, *mchod chog*) and an offering-practice ritual (drub chö, *sgrub mchod*) are terms Kongtrul seems to use interchangeably in many cases in this text. An offering ritual usually refers to a ceremony of visualization of a specific deity or master and presentation of offerings. An offering-practice ritual for the deities of the highest level of tantra usually includes much more than offerings: meditation on oneself as the deity, on the deity before one, on the deity in a ceremonial vase, offerings, self-empowerment, and a vajra feast.

Below, at the end of the section entitled "The Monthly Program of Memorial Offerings and Extra Rituals," Kongtrul makes a distinction between these two rituals; elsewhere he has not used the terms consistently.

[11] In tantric meditations deities are often arranged in a particular geometric (usually circular) configuration (kyil kor, *dkyil 'khor*). For example, there are five deities in the configuration of the Five Tantric Deities: one figure in the center of a circle (*dkyil*), surrounded by four others on the circumference (*'khor*).

[12] The Original School of Translation refers to those translations begun at the time of Guru Rinpochay's visit to Tibet during the ninth century. The Later School of Translation refers to translations begun subsequent to Atisha's arrival in Tibet during the eleventh century.

[13] The New Treasures (Ter Sar, *gter gsar*) does not refer to any specific set of texts. It refers to treasure teachings discovered during the era of the author, in this case the nineteenth century. In the present day, only treasure texts revealed during the twentieth century would be referred to as New Treasures.

- All texts that are recited [during the course of] the torma ceremony on the twenty-ninth [day of the lunar month], including *Vermillion*
- The main and supplementary texts for the ritual [to offer] torma to the Six-Armed Protector (Mahakala; Chag Drukpa, *phyag drug pa*)
- [Various texts for protector rituals,] including *The General Torma Offering to the Committed Protectors,* and ones for Mantra Protectress, the Mamo of the Charnel Ground, and Goddess of Longevity from the New Treasures

You must also have the following instruction manuals:

- The main and supplementary texts from the Shangpa Instruction Lineage for the preliminary and main practices of the Six Doctrines of Niguma in both [the Jonang] and Tang Tong Gyalpo traditions
- *Great Seal: The Ocean of Certainty* and the supplementary text that elucidates it
- *The Stages of the Path for the Three Types of Individuals*
- *The Seven Points of Mind Training*
- [The instructions for the Shangpa practices] of the two traditions of Great Seal of the Amulet Box, the three Meditations-in-Action, Deathlessness and Non-Entering, the Inseparability of the Spiritual Master and the Protector, and the two texts [practice and commentary] of the Integrated Practice of the Four Deities
- *Meaningful to Behold*, which contains the instructions for the preliminary and main practices of Wheel of Time and the Six Branches of Application
- The instructions for the Great Perfection practice of the Innermost Essence of the Spiritual Master, including the preliminary practices and the supplication to the lineage

- The cycle of [rituals of] the activity of vajra feasts,[14] the instruction manuals, etc., of Severance in the Zurmang [tradition]
- The main text and the daily practice of White Tara, Wish-Fulfilling Wheel

All these books are in print so you must make sure to procure them before [the retreat]. A few minor texts (including the Six-Armed Protector [meditation] of the New Treasures) are not in print: you must copy these by hand before the time they are to be used [during the retreat program].

The retreatant of the protector temple must be sure to have the following texts:

- All the texts for recitation and the instruction manuals for the phases of creation and completion of the Gathering of the Jewels
- All the recited texts and manuals for the Gathering of the Joyful Ones of the Eight Great Configurations of Deities, for [Black] Lord of Life of the New Treasures, and for whatever other practices are necessary.

As the time to enter retreat approaches you should make a thousand or more *tsa-tsas* containing long mantras, circumambulate the precious upper and lower temples a thousand times, and make as many offerings (of lamps, etc.) as possible.[15] If you have some wealth, you should offer tea and food to the virtuous community or present food and

---

[14] A vajra feast (tsok, *tshogs*) is an offering made to the deities and the participants in meditations of the highest tantras. Anything edible may be offered but the obligatory ingredients of a vajra feast are meat and alcohol.

[15] *Tsa-tsas* are small clay models of stupas. They contain long mantras (zung, *gzungs*), literally "reminders." The words of these prayers are meant to remind the reader of the import of spiritual instructions.

Circumambulation by walking in a clockwise direction around stupas or temples is a common practice among Buddhists in the Himalayan region. The upper and lower precious temples mentioned here are the main temple of Palpung Monastery and, situated above, the retreat center affiliated with it.

money to four pure fully ordained persons. If you are not wealthy, you should at least occasionally offer a noon meal to a pure, faith-inspiring monk or nun. During all of these activities you should pray that you will complete your retreat without any interruptions and that the instructions for spiritual development will become integrated with your stream of experience. You should do whatever possible to accumulate a mass of virtuous activities, including repairing roads or footpaths, if appropriate; ransoming the lives [of animals from the butcher] and releasing them; and giving gifts to the poor. These are crucial forms of virtue and very significant acts in both the short and long terms. Therefore, the retreat director, the vajra master,[16] should first arrange these [activities for you] and [then] they should be done a number of times.

ENTRANCE INTO RETREAT

You should spend a day [prior to the retreat] offering as many water tormas[17] as possible. This practice should be performed with the cleanliness and purity stipulated.

You should offer the best ceremonial scarves that you are able to afford in both the Great Glorious Temple and the protector temple in the retreat center.[18] Then for a period of a week, you should perform the intensive practice of the single form of Vajra Youth of the Secret Vital Essence cycle of the New Treasures.[19] This will subdue obstacles and

[16] The vajra master (dorjay lobpon, *rdo rje slob dpon*) was Kongtrul's representative as director of the retreat and its principal instructor in his absence.

[17] Water tormas (chu tor, *chu gtor*) are offerings of water and grain presented to gods of wealth and to the starving spirits. This practice was done every morning during the retreat.

[18] There were two temples in the retreat enclosure. One was used only for rituals addressed to the protectors; the other for all other occasions. This latter one, the larger of the two, was called Temple of the Great Glorious One (Palchen Lhakang, *dpal chen lha khang*). Its name derives from one of the deities of the Eight Great Configurations of Deities who was said to have a particularly strong presence in that area, Great Glorious Yangdak Heruka.

[19] The word for intensive practice in Tibetan, nyenpa (*bsnyen pa*), implies

interruptions [to your meditation practice]. You should also perform offering rituals [for the protectors of both] the Ancient and Later Schools during three days in the protector temple. You must be sure to do these practices and recitations even though they are not considered part of the main program of the retreat and are not counted within the three-year, three-fortnight period. Each person is responsible for providing for himself [or herself during those days] of retreat.

On the morning of an astrologically propitious [date], copious offerings of food are made to the gods according to *The Great Fragrant Smoke Offering of Gar*.[20] During the afternoon, following the completion of this ritual, *The Three-Part Torma Offering* should be made at the gate of the retreat center. The list of retreatants will then be posted. At this time, it should include the names of the eight persons from the monastery who [will enter the retreat] at the end of each year to ensure the continuity of the mantras during the protector torma practice. After [the posting of this list of names], no one else, high or low, is allowed to step inside the retreat center, except the cook [later referred to as "the retreat attendant"] and the woodsman.

---

familiarization, associating with, or approaching. In modern tantric practice the initial association with or approach to the deity is generally taught to be primarily verbal: the recitation of mantras. Some might argue that this is not the correct approach but it remains standard practice to measure deity meditation, as Kongtrul does in this book, by the numbers of mantras repeated.

When a meditation is said to be on the single form (chak gya chikpa, *phyag rgya gcig pa*), this indicates that there are no surrounding deities in that version of the meditation. The expression "single form" does not imply that the deity is alone: in this case, as with the other "single form" deities mentioned in this text, the deity is imagined in sexual union.

[20] A fragrant smoke (song, *bsang*) offering is prepared with branches of evergreen trees to produce a sweet-smelling smoke. The smoke carries the offerings to the gods or others. Smoky fires lit to welcome visiting lamas in the traditional manner belong to this category of burnt offering.

II. Life Within Retreat

There are five parts [to the description] of the training within the retreat center:

1. the specific meditation practices done during the three years and three fortnights
2. the daily program of four periods of meditation
3. the extra ceremonies that must be performed on a yearly or monthly basis[21]
4. the meditations and recitation practices [to be done] by the lama of the protector temple
5. a general description of the rules of conduct and discipline.

---

[21] The order of numbers two and three have been switched from that of the original text, both here and in the body of the translation below.

1. The Main Program of the Retreat

THE PRELIMINARY PRACTICES

The Origin of the Oral Instruction Lineage of the Karmapas

The retreat program begins with a series of meditations from the Oral Instruction Lineage of the Karmapas — the preliminary practices that precede meditation on Great Seal. The Oral Instruction Lineage traces its Tibetan origins to Marpa, the eleventh-century master who journeyed to India in search of instruction in meditation. Among his many teachers, it was the Indian yogi Maitripa who introduced him to Great Seal meditation. Maitripa's lineage began with another Indian named Ratnamati, who received instruction from the Buddha Vajra Holder on a non-physical plane. These instructions were then passed from master to disciple: from Ratnamati to Saraha, to Nagarjuna, to Shawaripa, and finally to Maitripa.

Once Great Seal meditation instructions arrived in Tibet, their place within the Oral Instruction Lineage went through a gradual transformation. Milarepa, Marpa's main disciple, emphasized the Six Doctrines of Naropa (called "the path of means") in his teaching;

Gampopa, his foremost disciple, brought Great Seal meditation to the fore. As Kongtrul explains in *The Torch of Certainty*:

> The custom of the noble Milarepa was to give instruction first in the path of means since once a meditator has achieved stable experience of inner heat and illusory body, the essence of Great Seal meditation is realized naturally. The incomparable Dakpo [Gampopa] trained most of his disciples in the stages of the path according to the teachings of the Buddha's Word as Instruction Lineage. To his special disciples he taught a condensed version of the meditations of the path of means and then gave direct pointing-out instructions in Great Seal meditation. (previously unpublished in translation; page 51a in the Tibetan edition)

Gampopa succeeded in popularizing the Oral Instruction Lineage teachings: he made them accessible to persons of all capacities and wrote the early instruction manuals for the lineage. He brought the teachings down from Milarepa's Himalayan peaks to a monastic system where they have mostly remained ever since. If the present-day masters of the Oral Instruction Lineage do not resemble Marpa or Milarepa in appearance, lifestyle, or instruction, it is probably due to Gampopa's pervasive influence.

Gampopa was the last master of the entire lineage; he was followed by a deluge of major and minor subsects within the Oral Instruction Lineage. Each built a system of monastic institutions of its own, developed distinct liturgies and manuals for study and meditation, and became centered around one or many masters who provided continuity to the institutions and the scholastic and meditative traditions through a series of recognized incarnations.

One of these subsects, the Oral Instruction Lineage of the Karmapas, is centered around the succession of incarnations of a master named Dusum Kyenpa (Knower of the Past, Present, and Future), one of the main disciples of Gampopa. As Kongtrul relates in *An Impartial History of the Sources of Spiritual Instruction*:

> The second incarnation of Dusum Kyenpa called Chökyi Lama ["Master of Spiritual Instructions"; also known as Karma Pakshi] possessed renunciation and realization identical in every respect with that of the illustrious master Saraha. In aeons past he had been empowered by the buddhas in unison as the performer of their enlightened activity. His name, the glorious Karmapa ["Performer of Enlightened Activity"] became renowned throughout the oceans of pure realms of the great Highest Buddha Realm.

He revealed this name to his disciples in general, and for this reason [his lineage is called] the Oral Instruction Lineage of the Glorious Karmapa. Within the splendid mansion of the Buddha's doctrine in the Himalayan region, this great school represents the highest point, like the top of a victory banner.

[This lineage] is led by a father and his five spiritual sons. [The father is] the victor Karmapa, [embodiment of the bodhisattva] Powerful All-Seeing One, who has appeared in a series of fourteen incarnations. The enlightened activity of his lives of freedom is renowned throughout India, China, and the Tibetan Himalayas. The victor Shamarpa, [embodiment of] the protector Buddha Boundless Light [Amitabha], has appeared during his ten incarnations to be the disciple of this master but in fact he is essentially identical to [Karmapa] in his qualities of renunciation and realization.[22] Five incarnations of Goshri Gyaltsab, [the embodiment of the bodhisattva] Vajra-in-Hand [Vajrapani], have appeared (from [the first,] Paljor Döndrup, until Norbu Zangpo). The victor, [the bodhisattva] Loving-Kindness [Maitreya] [incarnate], Kenting Tai Situ, has appeared in six incarnations who possessed the eyes of the Buddha's teaching and six who possessed a lotus tongue.[23] As well, there have been the series of incarnations of the illustrious Pawo and Trayo Rinpochays.

This father [Karmapa] and five sons [Shamarpa, Goshri Gyaltsab, Tai Situpa, Pawo, and Trayo] were mentioned in various treasure texts by the great [master from] Oddiyana [Guru Rinpochay]. He also expressed abundant praise for their ability to place others on the stage of non-regression to cyclic existence through being seen, heard, or remembered or through their touch. These are not just words from a book:

---

[22] There is a hidden message in this praise of Shamarpa. What Kongtrul does not mention is that Shamarpa Mipam Chödrup Gyatso, a master of Kongtrul's principal master, lost his life in a dispute between Nepal and the central Tibetan government. As a result, formal recognition of reincarnations of this master was outlawed by the Tibetan government from 1792 until the 1960s.

[23] Kongtrul's calculation of the number of Tai Situpas differs from the modern standard. According to Kongtrul, his spiritual master, Payma Nyinjay Wangpo, was the twelfth Tai Situpa. *The Encyclopedia of Buddhism*, written after the recognition of Payma Nyinjay's incarnation, Payma Kunzang, mentions thirteen Tai Situpas. By this calculation the present Tai Situpa would be the fifteenth of that incarnation lineage, whereas he is usually counted as the twelfth. Except in this case, I have followed the modern system in ascribing numbers to the Tai Situs.

> these masters are not ordinary persons of limited experience devoid of outstanding qualities or unable to help others. Those among them who have appeared as scholars have been [of an erudition] identical with that of the great leaders of Indian Buddhism. Those among them who have appeared as meditators have not been satisfied with slight signs of success on the spiritual path but have attained the exalted state of great vajra masters. (pages 7b-8a)

The vitality of the Oral Instruction Lineage of the Karmapas derives in part from its embrace of many different systems of meditation within its structure. Many of its past and present leaders have centered their personal meditation practice on instructions far removed from those of Marpa. Even the main protector of the Karmapas, Vajra Black-Caped One, is a newcomer to the Oral Instruction Lineage, having originated in the treasure texts of the Ancient Instruction Lineage. Modern masters of the Oral Instruction Lineage of the Karmapas often give empowerments from other lineages: Vajrasattva, Buddha of Boundless Light, Garuda, Vajra Dagger (Vajra Kilaya) and many others from the Ancient Instruction Lineage; Wheel of Time from the Vajra Yoga Instruction Lineage; the introductory empowerment to the Severance Instruction Lineage; and Six-Armed Protector from the Shangpa Instruction Lineage, to name just a few. From the point of view of strict adherence to their roots in the Oral Instruction Lineage of Marpa, the leaders of this lineage appear to be somewhat unorthodox but this same expansive vision seems to have contributed to the lasting success of the tradition.

Manuals Used During the Preliminary Practices

Kongtrul mentions five manuals as guides for this stage of the retreat. The first two, and most important, are *Great Seal: The Ocean of Certainty* by the ninth Karmapa, Wangchuk Dorjay; and a supplementary text which he does not name. This latter text is probably *The Torch of Certainty* by Kongtrul himself, available to us in a translation by Judith Hanson (Boston: Shambhala, 1977).

The Ocean of Certainty is the longest of three texts on Great Seal meditation written by Wangchuk Dorjay. The middle-length text of the series, *The Mahamudra Eliminating the Darkness of Ignorance*, has been translated by Alexander Berzin (Dharamsala: Library of Tibetan Works and Archives, 1978). *The Ocean of Certainty* surpasses the scope of most guides to meditation: it was not written for a prospective meditator but for the master who must guide students from ordinary states of mind to full enlightenment. The text includes questions that the teacher should ask the meditator of his or her experience, Zen roshi-style, and provides advice on how to continue guiding the meditator based on the answers received. The author warns against letting the meditator read passages that are beyond his or her scope, in case familiarity with the teacher's manual might create obstacles to the meditator's progress. Kongtrul himself advises that instruction in this text be completed only during the stage of the retreat devoted to Great Seal practice. *The Ocean of Certainty* stands among the most inspiring books ever written in Tibetan but it is difficult to imagine a translation being made available to the general public.

Kongtrul wrote *The Torch of Certainty* as a supplement to *The Ocean of Certainty*. It contains instructions in the visualizations for the preliminary practices. It remains an indispensable text — both in its original and its translation — for all those who undertake the preliminary practices of this lineage.

The third manual is *The Jewel Ornament of Liberation* by Gampopa, translated in 1958 by Herbert V. Guenther (Boston: Shambhala, 1971). This venerable jewel, an introduction to Buddhism of the Great Way, was written in the twelfth century and is still required reading for any member of the Oral Instruction Lineage. The classical style of its language presents some difficulty for modern Tibetan readers and its dryness can be a source of boredom for modern non-Tibetan readers, particularly for those whose imaginations have soared with *The Hundred Thousand Songs of Milarepa*. The styles of the two books reflect the very different personalities and audiences of this master and disciple. Milarepa was a unique character: before meeting Marpa he had been a black magician and had murdered many people through his powers. He taught very few people during his lifetime; his teachings were oriented to those persons able to follow his example of total dedication to meditation and spiritual life. In contrast, Gampopa was a doctor and had entered a monastery only after the death of his wife. More a man used to serving all people, he wrote manuals such as this one to provide an entrance to the Oral Instruction Lineage for those of every capacity and circumstance.

The fourth manual mentioned, *The Stages of the Path for the Three Types of Individual* by Taranata, is another introduction to the Great Way from the Buddha's Word as Instruction (Kadampa) Lineage. The book is more practical than *Jewel Ornament* in that it guides the reader through three stages of refinement of the motivation to practice Buddhism. The motivation of the first type of individual is focused on improving his or her situation in this life or the next. The second aspires to leave cyclic existence altogether; the third, to attain enlightenment for the sake of all living beings. Unfortunately this book is unavailable in foreign languages.

The Great Path of Awakening, another manual from the Buddha's Word as Instruction Lineage, is not mentioned by name in this text, but Kongtrul refers the retreatants to a commentary on *The Seven Points of Mind Training* and I have assumed that he intends that they should read his own work. Kongtrul wrote this book in 1854, six years before the beginning of the first retreat under his supervision. This work, translated by Ken McLeod (Boston: Shambhala, 1987), is situated on the borderline of tantric meditations: while the main topic of the book is the system of mind training of the Great Way, the book introduces a meditation on the spiritual master and a visualization called taking and sending that anticipate tantric meditation techniques.

The Buddha's Word as Instruction Lineage

The last three books mentioned above — *The Jewel Ornament of Liberation*, *The Stages of the Path for the Three Types of Individual*, and *The Great Path of Awakening* — share a common source in the Buddha's Word as Instruction Lineage. On the subject of its origins, Kongtrul states:

> After [the Tibetan] King Lang Darma's suppression of Buddhism ended, Lhalama Ku'ön sent twenty-one young men, including the great translator Rinchen Zangpo, to India. They invited the glorious lord Atisha [to Tibet]. Through the kindness of this master and the translator, an infinite number of profound teachings from the Buddha's discourses and tantras were newly translated. [Translations done] from this time forth are known as Later Translations of new tantras.
>
> Of Lord Atisha's three principal disciples — Ku Tsöndru Yungdrung, Ngok Lekpay Sherab, and Dromton Gyalway Jungnay — the last had three main disciples — Putowa, Chen Ngawa, and Puchungwa — known as the three brothers. A disciple of the first, Langri Tangpa Dorjay Sengay, was the actual embodiment of the Buddha Boundless Light. These and many other outstanding bodhisattva masters who resembled *arhants* appeared [in this lineage] and liberated an infinite number of people through their instruction in the stages of the path for three types of individual. This lineage is known as the Buddha's Word as Instruction Lineage.

> Previously there were many monastic centers associated with this lineage.... Now, however, this lineage's instructions have become blended with the systems of training native to the institutions of the Kagyu, Gayluk, Sakya and other traditions.... Apart from this [continuity of the teachings], the lineage has maintained no distinct institutions. (*ibid*, pages 5b-6a)

The spiritual masters of the Buddha's Word as Instruction Lineage are remembered for their unflinching self-examination and scrupulous honesty. They dedicated themselves wholeheartedly to spiritual life. One of their famous sayings advises:

> Turn your innermost attention to the instructions for spiritual development.
> Once you have embraced spiritual life, live as a beggar.
> In living as a beggar, decide to die as one.
> When dying, do so without companions.
> Leave human society.
> Join the ranks of dogs.
> Attain the rank of an enlightened one.

This sort of attitude won the lineage universal respect and admiration but few adherents. Its practice centers fell into disuse and its teachings found new, more opulent homes in other monastic systems.

The Importance of the Preliminary Practices

Kongtrul emphasizes the importance of the preliminary practices within the retreat program. The preliminary practices are well known to tantric Buddhists, but not well loved. They are often regarded as the arduous, unavoidable price one has to pay to arrive at the "real" and somewhat more glamorous practices just over the horizon. While it is true that these are preliminary to what are called the "main" practices of the creation and completion phase meditations, they precede the latter in the same way that filling a vehicle's fuel tank precedes a long journey. Tantric meditations are like a luxurious and powerful car; the preliminary practice training in disengagement from worldly concerns, in compassion, and in devotion to the spiritual master are like fuel. Without this preparatory training, the splendid car with an empty tank goes nowhere. Kongtrul explains why this is so by quoting a master from the Shangpa Lineage:

As the great Sang-gyay Nyenton said, the following is extremely important during both the preliminary and main practices:

> Among all essential meditation instructions, three reign supreme. [First,] develop a helpful and loving attitude by undertaking all activity out of compassion. [Second,] concentrate continually and intensely on impermanence and death to the point that your preoccupations diminish and you feel you need nothing whatsoever. [Third,] pray whole-heartedly to your spiritual master so that extraordinary devotion wells up within you. Develop this unceasing devotion to your spiritual master to the point of crying unfeignedly.
>
> These three will cause the spontaneous awareness of the illusory nature of one's experience; all appearing phenomena to seem unreal; spontaneous lucid dreams during which one can act freely, multiply [appearances], emanate [forms], transform [appearances], or actually discern a specific place; the arising of the clear, non-discursive state of Great Seal during the day; and the spontaneous appearance of oneself as the deity or the arising of boundless radiant awareness during the night. All of these experiences will arise exactly as they are described [in meditation texts].
>
> If you have not developed the three points mentioned above it will be difficult for you to achieve the ultimate results of [tantric] meditation even by practicing intensely over a long period of time. Therefore it is essential to practice these three points firmly and wholeheartedly.

In this and other teachings he stressed these three points — compassion, impermanence, and devotion — and explained why it is indispensable [for a meditator] to always keep them in mind. (*The Prayers to be Recited*, pages 7a-b)

This is the mental training which lies at the heart of the preliminary practices. Different styles of preliminary practices are repeated in an abbreviated form at different stages of the retreat. The reason for this is explained in one book that Kongtrul mentions later in this text, *The Ornament of the Guru's Mind*, by Rikzin Tsaywang Norbu:

> In brief, the best thing for you to do is to precede whatever practice of the phase of creation or completion you undertake

> with taking refuge, development of the mind of awakening, a set of one hundred thousand prostrations, a set of one hundred thousand repetitions of the hundred-syllable mantra, a set of one hundred thousand offerings of the universe, and a set of one hundred thousand supplications [to the spiritual master]. If these practices have first been done, their force will prevent obstacles and will produce rapid results during the meditations of the main practices. These practices have the capability of yielding the fruit of [later meditations] exactly as described in the practice texts. (pages 19b-20)

The Retreat Program for the Preliminary Practices

The first practice is of four reflections: on the difficulty of obtaining this free and bountiful [human life]; on impermanence and death; on actions, causes, and effects; and on the shortcomings of [life lived within the bounds of] cyclic existence. Three days are spent reflecting on each of these subjects. These contemplations, as well as the four preliminary practices — one hundred thousand repetitions of the refuge prayer, of the hundred-syllable [mantra of Vajrasattva], of [an offering] of the universe in a symbolic form, and of [the supplication of the practice] of uniting with the mind of the spiritual master[24] — must all be finished within a period of five months.

When convenient [during this time,] you should become familiar with the contents of *The Jewel Ornament of Liberation* by the incomparable doctor from Dakpo [Gampopa]; *Great Seal: The Ocean of Certainty* by the ninth lord [Karmapa, Wangchuk Dorjay,] and its supplementary text; and *The Stages of the Path for the Three Types of Individuals* by the great noble one of Jonang [Taranata]. [Of these three,] *Great Seal: The Ocean of Certainty* should serve as the basic text and be taught in detail. The other two should be taught in the course of reading transmissions that support one's practice.[25]

---

[24] Uniting with the mind of the spiritual master approximates a literal translation of the Tibetan term *bla ma'i rnal 'byor* (pronounced "lamay naljor"), also commonly translated as "guru yoga."

[25] In the course of a reading transmission (loong, *lung*), a master will read

Between periods of meditation at this time, the vajra master should give a commentary on the Indian Buddhist source texts *Fifty Verses in Praise of the Spiritual Master*, *Twenty Verses on the Bodhisattva Vow*, and *The Fourteen Root Downfalls*. He should also give instruction in and an explanation of the combined root text and commentary of *The Twenty-five Vows*[26] by Garwang Chökyi Wangchuk.

The retreatants, for your part, should recite *The Twenty-five Vows* each morning when convenient. You should recite it slowly while considering the meaning of the words. [In the morning,] the words at the end of the verses should be those of making a commitment, as in, "I will not forsake [the vow of] refuge in thought or deed." In the evening (at the end of the period of meditation at dusk, for example) you should [again] recite this prayer while doing prostrations, changing the words to those of acknowledgement of faults, as in, "I acknowledge having forsaken [the vow of] refuge in thought and deed." You should conscientiously examine whether or not you have incurred any physical, verbal, or mental faults or downfalls in the three disciplines during the day. If any have been incurred, you should sincerely acknowledge all of them with regret and commit yourself to not repeat them in the future. This is really crucial: you should be wholehearted in your training and act accordingly.

In the past the great virtuous guides of the Buddha's Word as Instruction Lineage would collect a white pebble for each virtuous thought that ran through their minds, or a black pebble for each unvirtuous thought. In the beginning the black stones were in the majority at the end of each day. Later the white and black stones were of equal numbers. Finally, there were only white stones. At that point they considered themselves as having entered the ranks of

---

a text aloud, often at high speed. The act of hearing this recitation, even if unintelligible to the listener, is considered to be an important part of the introduction to any subject within Buddhism, including meditation. In this retreat the vajra master would often combine a reading transmission and instruction on the meaning of a text.

[26] Kongtrul elsewhere sometimes refers to this text by the name *The Ocean of the Doctrine*.

persons who had genuinely embraced spiritual life. Some later great individuals recorded in writing the day's virtuous or unvirtuous thoughts and deeds as they occurred. In the evening, they would examine the list and would acknowledge [their faults] and commit [themselves to not repeat them]. While it may not be possible for you to do [as these persons did], your stream of experience should become slightly purified through your exercise of care and mindfulness. If not, you can't be considered a person on the spiritual path and your meditation practice will be without a heart.

During the practice of taking refuge and developing the mind of awakening, you should receive the two traditions' commitment to develop the mind to its full awakening if you have not already accepted it.[27] In connection to this [commitment], the instruction and explanation of *The Seven Points of Mind Training* [will be given]. From that point on, for as long as you live, you should never forget the training of the practice [described in] this instruction manual [*The Great Path of Awakening*]. Even if you don't manage to develop stable experience in other creation and completion phase meditations, you should be sure to make these teachings the central focus of your mental life. Don't forget them when happy and don't lose hold of them when depressed, during misfortune, or in other times of need when they should be applied.

Starting at the beginning of the practice of refuge, you must gradually complete one hundred thousand prostrations.

---

[27] Two traditions of the ritual for accepting the commitments of the mind of awakening were spread in Tibet: one has its origins with the Indian master Asanga, the other with the Indian master Shantideva. See *The Jewel Ornament of Liberation*, pages 118-37, for details of both rituals.

THE SHANGPA INSTRUCTION LINEAGE

The Origin of the Lineage

The next fifteen months of the retreat are devoted to meditations from the Shangpa Instruction Lineage. This lineage is a rarity among the world's living spiritual traditions: it finds its source in the teachings of two very remarkable women, Niguma and Sukasiddhi. These two women of eleventh-century India attained such heights of realization that they each received instruction directly from the buddha of the tantras, Vajra Holder. Tibetan texts do not record any meeting between these two women of supreme accomplishment. Their teachings live side-by-side today because they shared a disciple, a Tibetan by the name of Kyungpo Naljor. This extraordinary yogi-monk gathered instructions from 150 teachers — some scholars, some meditation masters; some women, some men — during many journeys to India and Nepal. The collection of the teachings he brought back to Tibet and passed on to others is what is now known as the Shangpa Instruction Lineage (Shang is a place name). Central to this system are the teachings of these two women who are now remembered as two of the greatest meditation masters Buddhist India produced.

The identity of Niguma remains veiled by a quirk of Tibetan language: the honorific words for "wife" and "sister" are identical. Niguma is mentioned in many texts as the *cham-mo (lcam mo)* of Naropa: does that word here refer to her as a wife or as a sister of the famous Indian scholar-turned-yogi? The word smiles inscrutably from the page.

What is certain is that she surpassed her more renowned brother or husband. While his spiritual apprenticeship lasted an arduous twelve years, Niguma attained spiritual awakening in just one week and far exceeded the stage of awakening of all but a very few before or after her in that she received a large corpus of instruction directly from the Buddha on a non-physical plane. As Taranata states in *A Supplement to the History of the Lineages*:

> The account of the wisdom dakini Niguma as the sister/wife of Naropa, etc. is well-known everywhere. It should be added that she received a few instructions from the master Lawapa of the East. After meditating with the master for one week, she became a wisdom dakini exhibiting a rainbow-like physical form and spiritual realization which reached the eighth stage of awakening. It is said that Lawapa of the East's body dissolved into light, leaving only a palm-sized portion of the crown of his head behind. He was also known as Lawapa the Younger.

> She is known as Nigu, Nigupta in Sanskrit, said to mean definite secret or definitely hidden, although the name is really from the symbolic language of the dakinis. From her, the great accomplished Kyungpo Naljor, who possessed the five ultimate qualities, received many of the tantric transmissions known throughout the noble land [of India]. In particular, her special instructions included the great empowerment of the illusory body which she bestowed on him on the night of the fifteenth of the fourth lunar month, by the light of the full moon. The following morning she taught him the entire Six Doctrines in his dreams: he was later to receive these instructions from her in waking life twice, a total of three times. (pages 2b-3a)

Niguma is remembered as being playful as well as fully enlightened: on her first meeting with Kyungpo Naljor, she claimed to be the chief of a group of cannibal witches and advised Kyungpo to run for his life before her coven arrived to feast on him. When she threw away his offering of gold, he began to wonder if she were telling the truth! But he didn't panic; and the rest, as they say, is history.

Niguma's copious teachings make up the bulk of the Shangpa Instruction Lineage but it is her contemporary, Sukasiddhi, who is considered the figure whose continuing influence sustains and nourishes the lineage. Sukasiddhi had been a housewife until she was thrown out of her house by her irate husband and children: expecting them to return home with money or food, she had given what little they had to a beggar. Already fifty-nine years old, she wandered destitute and alone until she managed to sell some beer she had brewed. She became a brewer and merchant and eventually made gifts of beer to a local yogi, the great accomplished master Virupa. He offered to give her empowerment and instruction, which she gratefully accepted. In the course of a single evening, she attained enlightenment; her body was transformed from that of a sixty-one-year-old to that of a rainbow-like appearance of a young woman. Like Niguma, she attained such a high level of realization that she received instruction directly from the Buddha Vajra Holder on a non-physical plane.

When Kongtrul wrote the ritual for offering to the masters of the Shangpa Instruction Lineage, he placed Sukasiddhi in the center of that assembly. It is to her that most praises and offerings are addressed and from her that empowerment is received at the conclusion of the ceremony. Kyungpo Naljor considered her the kindest of all his spiritual masters, one reason being that she promised to continue to bless and sustain the holders of his lineage. Niguma herself contributed to the renewal of the lineage by appearing in later centuries to Tang Tong Gyalpo on three occasions and to Kunga Drolchok twice, imparting many instructions to both.

Kyungpo Naljor's exceptionally long life of 150 years (978-1127) made him a contemporary of many of the great early masters of the later spread of Buddhism in the Himalayan region. He had practiced and gained realization in both the pre-Buddhist Tibetan religion called Bön and the Ancient Instruction Lineage before setting out for Nepal and India in search of more instructions. Of the 150 masters he found, Niguma, Sukasiddhi, Maitripa, Rahula, and Dorjay Denpa were the main contributors to what became known as the Shangpa Instruction Lineage.

Kongtrul had this opinion of Kyungpo Naljor, expressed in *An Impartial History of the Sources of Spiritual Instruction*:

> His attainment of accomplishment equalled that of the Indian masters Luyipa, Krishnacharya, and Ghantapa. In the Tibetan region it would seem that among the twenty-five disciples [of Guru Rinpochay] during the original [spread of Buddhism] or [among the masters] of this later period, no one has ever appeared who equalled his mastery of scholastic erudition, accomplishment in meditation, miraculous powers, and enlightened activity. (page 11b)

The Main Meditations of the Lineage

Kongtrul included most of the main meditations from the Shangpa Instruction Lineage in his retreat program; most of these originated with Niguma.

The creation phase meditations that form the basis of the practices focus on deities known as Wheel of Supreme Bliss and The Five Tantric Deities. The latter is a practice unique to this lineage: five of the main deities of the Highest Yoga Tantra are present in a single configuration. These deities represent the ultimate expressions of five subjects taught in the tantras; Kyungpo Naljor was considered to be the embodiment of them all. Kongtrul explains this in *The Encyclopedia of Buddhism*:

> The ultimate expression of inner heat is Adamantine Joy [Hevajra]; the ultimate expression of action seal, Wheel of Supreme Bliss [Chakrasamvara]; the ultimate expression of illusory body and clear light, Quintessential Secret [Guhyasamaja]; the ultimate expression of dream, Great Illusion [Mahamaya]; and the ultimate expression of enlightened activity, Terrifying Vajra [Vajra Bhairava].

> [Kyungpo Naljor] was able to actually reveal [to others] these Five Tantric Deities at the five places of his body. (Volume 1, page 534)

The completion phase meditations of the "Five Golden Doctrines" (so-called because Kyungpo Naljor offered gold to Niguma when requesting them) follow these deity meditations. These five are likened to the form of a tree. The roots of the five are the Six Doctrines of Niguma — meditations on inner heat, illusory body, dream, clear light, transference of consciousness, and the intermediate state. The trunk of the tree growing from these roots is meditation on Great Seal; Niguma's instructions are known as Great Seal of the Amulet Box. There is no symbolic meaning to the name "amulet box": Kyungpo Naljor wrote down Niguma's basic teachings on a palm leaf and kept it as a treasure in a sandalwood amulet box. The branches of the Five Golden Doctrines are the Three Meditations-in-Action: meditations on the spiritual master, the deity, and illusory body. The flowers are meditations on two dakinis, White and Red Celestial Women. Finally, the fruit of Niguma's system of meditation is Deathlessness and Non-Entering (of either cyclic existence or perfect peace). In this retreat program, Niguma's instructions are followed by the Six Doctrines of Sukasiddhi and the longevity practices of these two inspirers of the lineage.

One week at the end of the first year of the retreat is spent meditating on a practice from this lineage, the Integrated Practice of the Four Deities. At the end of the second year, a week is spent meditating on the protector of this lineage, Six-Armed Protector. Both of these practices first appeared in Tibet through Kyungpo Naljor, who received them from Maitripa and Rahula. The annual year-end week-long practice of Six-Armed Protector also originates in the Shangpa lineage.

One of the special features of this system is that each stage of meditation is preceded by an empowerment: in comparison, a meditator is introduced to the Six Doctrines of Naropa by reading transmissions alone. The empowerments of Niguma's system are more accurately called "blessing ceremonies" and are translated below as "empowerment-blessings." Within the tantras of the Later Schools, five kinds of introductory initiations empower the disciple to begin a specific tantric meditation: empowerment, blessing, permission, introduction to awareness, and reading transmission. As Kongtrul explains in *A Concise Classification of Empowerments, Blessings and Related Ceremonies*:

> The second, blessing, confers the essence of the bestowal of empowerment in a concise form. While it conveys the entire

> meaning of the four empowerments, it does not include the actual ceremony of the four empowerments.... A blessing ceremony consists of few words and is easily performed. (page 5b)

> Most of the instructions for the profound doctrines of the glorious Shangpa Instruction Lineage consist entirely of the four empowerments within [the framework of] a blessing ceremony. From among those, the six instructions to the main practices of the Six Doctrines and others [are conferred by] meditation on radiating and absorbing [lights]: no material implement of empowerment whatsoever is used [in the course of the ceremony]. (page 6a)

Later History of the Lineage

The Shangpa Instruction Lineage spread far and wide in the Himalayan region without maintaining an institutional structure of its own. Masters associated with other lineages or affiliated with any monastic institution have become lineage holders of this tradition. During the nineteenth century it was Kongtrul, of the Oral Instruction Lineage of the Karmapas, and Jamyang Kyentsay, a reincarnate master of the Sakya monastic network, who were responsible for revitalizing the teachings of this lineage. During much of the twentieth century one of Kongtrul's reincarnations, Kalu Rinpochay of the Oral Instruction Lineage of the Karmapas, did much to further the availability of the Shangpa instructions to modern students of meditation in the Himalayan region and beyond.

None of these modern masters attempted to give this lineage an institutional structure: no Shangpa Instruction Lineage monasteries have been planned or built for many centuries. The lineage seems to live comfortably in retreat centers and in relative obscurity, often being mistaken for one of the lesser schools of the Oral Instruction Lineage.

The Shangpa Instruction Lineage was born of great promise: two of the most extraordinary masters of Buddhist India imparted their instructions to the person whom Kongtrul considered to be the greatest master Tibet ever produced. That the promise of the early days of the Shangpa Instruction Lineage did not fade with time is borne out by two assessments. The first is by Taranata in the early seventeenth century:

> Although the Shangpa Instruction Lineage has spread into countless lines of masters, there has never been a divergence between the words [of the instructions] and their meaning

> because of the firm seal of the dakinis' words. Since it is free of any contaminating embellishments, the Shangpa Instruction Lineage stands at the highest point above all lineages of meditation practice. (*Supplement*, pages 3a-b)

The second is by Kongtrul in the mid-nineteenth century, from *The Encyclopedia of Buddhism*:

> This instruction lineage has three special features that distinguish it as superior to all others. [First,] the holders of the lineage have been particularly outstanding individuals. The series of lineage masters is made up exclusively of bodhisattvas in their final lives [before attaining buddhahood]; this line has not been interrupted by the presence of ordinary individuals. [Second,] the meditation instructions themselves are particularly outstanding. Their meaning is not misleading and the words themselves are unpolluted: the vajra words of the verses sealed by the dakinis have never been altered by the compositions or embellishments of ordinary persons' imaginations. [Third,] the spiritual influence [of this lineage] is particularly outstanding. Even now, at the most extreme period of a degenerate age, its influence is such that [through its practices] the fruit of accomplishment will ripen for diligent persons who have kept the tantric commitments. (Volume 1, pages 237-38)

The Retreat Program for the Shangpa Instruction Lineage Meditations

Once the preliminary practices [described above] have been completed, [three empowerments] are bestowed: The first is the two-day great empowerment of the Five Tantric Deities of the Shangpa tradition — the preparation and the actual empowerment [each take one day]. The second, the first instruction that opens the door to blessings, is the empowerment of the five deities [in the configuration] of Wheel of Supreme Bliss. In this case the preparation and the actual empowerment are given together. The last of the three empowerments is the second instruction that opens the door to blessings, the empowerment of the meditative absorption of the five deities [of Wheel of Supreme Bliss].

Then the reading transmission for the practice text of the configuration of deities of Wheel of Supreme Bliss and a combined reading transmission and instruction for the meditation manual must be given. You then begin intensive practice on this meditation.

[During this practice,] the seven-syllable mantra [of the main deity] should be repeated seven hundred thousand times; the twenty-two syllable heart mantra, four hundred thousand times; the consort's mantra, one hundred thousand times; and the four dakinis' mantras, ten thousand times each. Every mantra [must be recited an extra number of times as] a complement. Then the offering practice is done for three, five, or seven days, as suitable; and the fire ritual to produce a pacifying effect is performed for three days to complete the practice.[28] [From start to finish,] this meditation must be completed within two months' time.

Two empowerments are then given: The first is the great empowerment of the illusory body (also called the Gate That Is the Source of All Qualities), the first instruction of the inner arrangement of blessings. This is followed by the second of that series, the empowerment of the meditative absorption of the Five Tantric Deities [in a configuration] that is condensed to include the central deities alone.

Once the reading transmission and the instruction for the meditation on the configuration of the central deities alone is given, the intensive practice of the Five Tantric Deities is done during one month. During this time, each [deity's] mantra must be recited one hundred thousand times, a total of five hundred thousand, plus a complement [of extra mantras]. The full offering practice is done at the end for just three days.

Following this, you begin the preliminary practices for the Six Doctrines of Niguma. The instructions from the main lineage of Shangpa teachings (the Jonang tradition) and those of the direct lineage of Tang Tong Gyalpo are given

---

[28] During a fire ritual (jin sek, *sbyin sreg*; literally "burnt offering"), offerings are made to the deities imagined in the fire. Such rituals can be done with the intention that the effect of the offerings and meditations be any one of the four forms of enlightened activity. The visualizations, mantras, and offerings vary according to the effect desired.

concurrently. You then meditate on the Empty Enclosure of Ah for one week.

This is followed by the meditation of inner heat, the first of the six doctrines of the stream of blessings. Once you have received the empowerment-blessing and the instructions for the visualizations, you meditate on the wild-fire [stage] of inner heat for three weeks. At this point you should learn the physical exercises of Naropa and Niguma and do them daily at a convenient time, without missing a day. The main part of the practice, consuming the food [of inner heat], lasts for two months. The three months spent meditating on inner heat are ended by a week's training in the instructions from the very direct lineage, [the accomplishment of] inner heat in a single sitting.

Then, as you receive the appropriate empowerment-blessings and instructions in the visualizations, you meditate on illusory body, clear light, and dream for three weeks each, and on transference of consciousness and intermediate state for two weeks each. Because the time [devoted to each meditation] is very limited, you should practice [assiduously, to the extent of] producing some signs of success. At the end of each practice the visualizations for the "single sitting" instructions should be given in their entirety.

Following these practices, the empowerment-blessing for the meditation of Great Seal of the Amulet Box is given and its practice is done for two months. The blessing for the Jonang tradition instruction which introduces you to the nature of mind, the Means to Attain the Body of Wisdom, should be given [during these months] whenever appropriate, and the instruction and reading transmission for the main part of *Great Seal: The Ocean of Certainty* should be completed.

Then the empowerment-blessings for Meditation-in-Action of the spiritual master and the meditation deity are given and you maintain the three meditations-in-action for a period of a week. (The blessing [for the third,] Meditation-in-Action of the illusory body, is identical with that of illusory body within the Six Doctrines so it is unnecessary to repeat it at this time.)

Following this practice, the empowerment-blessings for White Celestial Woman and the three celestial women together are given. ([The blessing for] Red Celestial Woman is identical to [that which was given] for transference of consciousness so it is not repeated at this point.) Once the reading transmission and instructions have been given, you meditate on White and Red Celestial Women for ten days each, reciting one hundred thousand of their mantras during each period. [During this time,] you should train in the stage of completion of these meditations, transference of consciousness, until the signs of success appear.

Then, after the empowerment-blessing and instructions are given, Deathlessness of Body and Mind and Non-Entering [of both perfect peace and cyclic existence] are meditated upon for a week. Following this, the empowerment-blessing and instructions for the practice of the Inseparability of the Spiritual Master and the Protector is given and the meditation and recitation of mantras are done during one week.

One month is then spent practicing [the Six Doctrines of Sukasiddhi]. The empowerment-blessing and instruction in the visualizations [for the meditation] of the wisdom dakini, Sukasiddhi, are given as a preliminary. [For the practice itself], the creation phase meditation and recitation [of the mantra] are done at the beginning of each meditation session for however long you wish. The four main doctrines are practiced for a week each; transference of consciousness and the intermediate state are meditated upon as supplementary practices.

Finally, the empowerments for the longevity practices of both Niguma and Sukasiddhi are given. As an assurance of virtuous good fortune, these two meditations should be done during one week.

This completes all the main practices of the Shangpa Instruction Lineage.

THE VAJRA YOGA INSTRUCTION LINEAGE

The Origin of the Lineage

The next six months of the retreat are devoted to the meditations from the Vajra Yoga Instruction Lineage. This lineage consists principally of the instructions for the creation phase meditation of the deity Wheel of Time and its associated completion phase meditations, the Six Branches of Application. The tantra of the Wheel of Time represents the ultimate teaching within the tantras of the Later Translation School. As Kongtrul states in *The Encyclopedia of Buddhism*:

> [The tantra of] the glorious Wheel of Time was taught by the Buddha in the year before he passed into the realm of perfect peace. On the full moon day of the black month (third of the lunar calendar), he travelled by the power of his enlightenment to the Dhanyakataka ["Treasure Mound"]Stupa in southern India. He emanated the configuration of Lord of Speech of Totality [i.e., Wheel of Time] below and that of the glorious constellations above, then assumed his seat on a vajra throne [supported by] lions. He imparted the root text of the king of tantras containing 12,000 verses to the fortunate circle of disciples, which included those assembled within the configurations; King Suchandra, who had requested the instruction; and ninety-six other kings.
>
> This account is based on the tradition generally accepted by Tibetan practitioners of Wheel of Time, including the all-knowing Rangjung Dorjay [the third Karmapa]. According to the great noble one of Jonang [Taranata] and his followers, this event took place in the year after the enlightenment of our teacher. (Volume 1, pages 370-71)
>
> The ideas that are concealed by vajra words within all the other concise highest tantras are clearly, unambiguously presented within the tantra of glorious Wheel of Time. (Volume 3, page 429)
>
> The Six Branches of Application connected to the Yoga of the Three Vajras represent the pith of all [the instructions for] the completion phase meditations that are clearly presented in common by all the extensive root tantras. They are the culmination of all the [instructions for] the creation and completion phase meditations taught in the Highest Yoga tantras. They stand at the summit of all yoga practices, as universally recognized in India and Tibet as the sun and moon. (Volume 1, page 548)

The king mentioned in the first quote, King Suchandra, was ruler of the kingdom of Shambhala, a large kingdom hidden from human sight to the northwest of India. This kingdom of Shambhala is intricately connected to the origins of the tantras of Wheel of Time, as Kongtrul explains in *The Empowerment of Entering as a Child*:

> The spiritual king, Suchandra, transcribed all [the Buddha's] teaching on the tantras of Wheel of Time into [some] volumes. He himself composed a 60,000-verse commentary on the root text of the tantra of Wheel of Time and commissioned sculptors to construct a 400-cubit model of the configuration of deities made from precious metals and jewels. He taught the Vajra Way of Secret Mantra extensively before his death. (page 6a)

He was succeeded by another Buddhist lineage bearer (as the kings were called) of Shambhala. The line continued exclusively within the kingdom until,

> during the time Dignaga and Chandrakirti were safeguarding the doctrine [in India], Lineage Bearer Abhaya-Vishnu travelled by his miraculous power to Kashmir. He stayed there for three months, erecting a stone pillar and imparting many instructions in the Vajra Way.... [Later,] the great Kalachakra-pada, Jampay Dorjay, the son of an [Indian] yogi, travelled northward as instructed by a meditation deity. On his way, he received instructions from an emanation of the lineage bearer [of Shambhala]. After having meditated for six months, he attained miraculous powers and was able to journey unhindered to Shambhala. There he met the lineage bearer himself and received the tantras of Wheel of Time and the three commentaries on them. Once he had memorized these, he returned to the noble land [of India] and imparted these instructions to Shri Badra (known as Lesser Kalachakra-pada) and others. These two masters taught innumerable accomplished masters: their instructions covered the earth. (*ibid*, pages 6a-b)

When examining the histories of the lineages of meditation instruction that reached the Himalayan region, we become accustomed to relatively tidy accounts of one Indian master's visit to Tibet and his designation of one main heir to his instructions, or of a single brave Tibetan who underwent the hardship of travel to India in search of instruction. In contrast, Kongtrul counts no less than seventeen different transmissions of the Vajra Yoga teachings that reached Tibet. The list of Indian masters involved in all these lineages reads like a Who's Who of the tantric masters of the later spread of Buddhist teachings to the Himalayas: it includes Shawaripa, Naropa, Atisha, and Shakya Shri.

It was a master of the thirteenth century who united all of these diverse transmissions, as Kongtrul relates:

> These seventeen traditions were received by a master of spiritual life and great renunciate, Shang Tukjay Tsöndru, an incarnation of a Shambhala lineage bearer. Counting his union of the existing transmissions and the instructions that he received of the tradition of the four disciples of the direct transmission of Bibuti, there were twenty distinct traditions in all. (*Encyclopedia*, Volume 1, page 551)

Tukjay Tsöndru (1243-1313) founded a monastery at Jonang in the western Tibetan region of Tsang and with it the Jonang tradition that Kongtrul regarded as the most important lineage of these teachings.

The Main Meditations of the Lineage

The Vajra Yoga Instruction Lineage is centered around the creation phase meditation of Wheel of Time and the completion phase meditations called the Six Branches of Application. Wheel of Time is the meditation deity whose tantra belongs to the Non-Dual Tantra, the pinnacle of the Highest Yoga Tantra. The empowerment that precedes this practice is called Entering as a Child. The stages of this empowerment are described in detail by the Dalai Lama and Jeffrey Hopkins in *The Kalachakra Tantra* (London: Wisdom, 1985).

The meditation on Wheel of Time is followed by a meditation on the three isolations — physical, verbal, and mental — a practice which precedes the Six Branches of Application.

The first of the Six Branches, withdrawal of the senses, has sometimes been translated correctly but misleadingly as individual withdrawal or individual convergence. As Taranata explains in *Meaningful to Behold*:

> In Sanskrit *prati* means individually, *ahara* can mean to gather, or to abandon, to eat, to sever, to receive, etc. Here it means to gather. Joining the two parts of the term, we have *pratyahara*, meaning to gather individually.... In brief, [the object of withdrawal of the senses is] to gather the ordinary appearances [which arise from each of the five senses] into the mind and to then experience the dawning of pure awareness. (page 15a)

Mental stability, the second branch, refers to the achievement of mastery of the previous meditation. The third branch, vitality control, has been translated elsewhere as vitality-stopping or life-effort. Taranata explains:

> In Sanskrit *prana* means life [or vitality]; *ayama* can mean to stop, effort, or to lengthen. Joining the two parts of the term, we have *pranayama*, meaning either life-effort or vitality-stopping. Here "life" refers to an energy wind; "stopping" and "effort" refer to making it enter [the central channel]. (*ibid*, page 26b)

The name of the fourth branch, retention, refers to preserving the flow of the energy wind into the central channel. The fifth, recollection, refers to integrating previous stages of meditation into the practice at this point. Taranata states:

> *Anusmriti* [in Sanskrit] means to recollect, to bring fully to mind. The previous meditations are recollected and kept firmly in mind. (*ibid*, page 38a)

The last of the six, meditative absorption [in Great Seal], represents the culmination of the path of Vajra Yoga. It is the practice of this meditation for three years and three fortnights that is said in the tantras of Wheel of Time to lead to enlightenment. As Taranata states:

> If this meditative absorption is maintained for three years and three fortnights once it has first arisen, the stage of the nature of ultimate reality will be definitively reached. At that point, the ordinary physical body dissolves into the sphere of totality and the body which is a manifestation of great wisdom is achieved. [This state in which awakening and its physical expression] are identical is the body of a great bodhisattva, complete with various qualities of awakening, such as the ten powers. (*ibid*, page 40b)

Later History of the Lineage

The Jonang Lineage as a distinct system of monastic institutions came to an abrupt end in 1648, fourteen years after the death of Taranata (1575-1634). One of Taranata's main sponsors was the ruler of Tsang, the western region of central Tibet. This was the time of the gathering of all of Tibet under the power of the fifth Dalai Lama; the Tsang ruler's resistance to changes in the power structure led to open warfare between his forces and troops under the Dalai Lama's command. The Tsang ruler was captured and put to death in 1642, ending most overt struggles in central Tibet. It would seem that strong anti-government feelings lingered in the monasteries for they were perceived as such a threat that all the Jonang tradition monasteries were forcibly absorbed into the Gayluk order. While political considerations were the underlying reason, the excuse given for the takeover was the claim that Taranata had been a corrupt master and his monastic system, by extension, corrupted. The name of his main residence, Takten Puntsok Ling, was changed to Ganden Puntsok Ling, after one of the main Gayluk monasteries in Lhasa. The entire religious life of all of his monasteries was transformed, the frescoes on the walls repainted, and some important works by Dolpo Sang-gyay (1292-1361), one of the early masters of the Jonang tradition whose philosophical views were an anathema to the Gayluk order, were locked up for over two hundred years until a contemporary of Kongtrul was able to secure their release.[29]

The hapless Shangpa Instruction Lineage had only recently become identified with the Jonang system of monasteries: Kunga Drolchok, Taranata's previous incarnation and head of the Jonang tradition, had received instructions from Niguma in visions and most of the modern source texts of the Shangpa Instruction Lineage were written by Taranata, based in part on those visions. In one stroke, then, both the Jonang and Shangpa institutions disappeared from the monastic map of the Himalayas. What are called the "four great schools" are the survivors of very worldly and sometimes bloody political struggles.

The Vajra Yoga and Shangpa instructions that had been the heart of the Jonang tradition survived the extinguishing of their institutions. The instructions were passed down in unbroken transmissions by a variety of masters usually identified with the Nyingma, Kagyu, or Sakya monastic systems. By including them in his retreat program, Kongtrul ensured that the instructions of the lineages remained vital, but he did nothing to revive the institutions. Although he never mentioned in his writings the events that led to the disappearance of these monastic systems, he took whatever opportunity he could to cite Dolpo Sang-gyay and Taranata, the two discredited Jonang masters, as two of the most reliable sources on almost any subject. Each time their names are mentioned, he underlined his faith in them by lavish but heartfelt praise. In the following quote Kongtrul refers to Dolpo Sang-gyay by the name of Sherab Gyaltsen Palzangpo:

---

[29] This is according to Gene Smith in his introduction to the Tibetan edition of *The Encyclopedia of Buddhism*, pages 34-35. Satapitaka series, vol. 80. Dehli: International Academy of Indian Culture, pp. 1-87.

> The foremost tradition [of Vajra Yoga] is the instruction lineage of the two[30] lineage bearers [of Shambhala]: [The first was] the omniscient master of spiritual life, Sherab Gyaltsen Palzangpo, whose understanding of the excellent teachings of the Buddha was characterized by the four ultimate reliances.[31] The life of this great master from Dolpo was foretold in *The Great Drum Discourse* and others, where a monk by the name of Muni ("Capable One") is mentioned. [The second was] the noble Taranata, a mighty upholder of the awakened conduct of accomplished masters of the past. He intentionally took rebirth during the lowest point of the age of dispute. Within the realm of profound secrets, he attained an exalted state equal to a second Buddha [of the tantras], Vajra Holder. The methods of practice [of Vajra Yoga] spread by these two masters are superior to all others: theirs is the central transmission within this lineage of meditation instructions. (*Encyclopedia*, Volume 1, page 552)

Taranata, the last holder of the Jonang tradition, had a particularly profound influence on Kongtrul's work. An indication of this can be found in the program of special yearly rituals for the retreat. Among all the masters of the past commemorated by a day of rituals, only Taranata's memorial day is observed by three consecutive days of collective rituals.

The Shangpa and Vajra Yoga Instruction Lineages were closely connected in the past; this affinity has continued to the present day. The main lineage holder of the Shangpa Instruction Lineage in recent years, the late Kalu Rinpochay, was the master requested by the sixteenth Karmapa to pass on the Vajra Yoga Instruction Lineage to the new generation of masters within the Oral Instruction Lineage of the Karmapas. Kalu Rinpochay also frequently bestowed the main empowerment of Wheel of Time from the Jonang tradition to Buddhists throughout the world. His main disciple, Bokar Tulku, continues this tradition: he is the retreat master at three retreat centers — that of Karmapa's monastery in Sikkim, the Shangpa retreat center at Kalu Rinpochay's monastery, and a Vajra Yoga retreat center at his own monastery.

---

[30] The text in Tibetan reads "the second" (*gnyis pa*) rather than "the two" (*gnyis*), which I assume is the correct version.

[31] The four reliances are to rely on the spiritual instruction, not the individual; to rely on the meaning, not the words; to rely on awakened awareness, not on ordinary consciousness; and to rely on definitive truth, not proximate truth.

The Intensive Practice Instruction Lineage

By the end of the first retreat, Kongtrul had decided to supplement the instructions of the Vajra Yoga Instruction Lineage with those from another lineage, the Intensive Practice Instruction Lineage. As he states in a book he wrote as the first retreat was ending:

> [During the three-year retreat here,] the meditations from the Vajra Yoga Instruction Lineage are [supplemented by instruction in the corresponding meditations from] the Intensive Practice of the Three Vajras Instruction Lineage. (*Catalogue*, page 90a)

The term *intensive practice* (nyen drup, *bsnyen sgrubs*) is used throughout tantric practice and is generally taught in four stages: familiarization, proximate practice, practice, and great practice. Kongtrul explains:

> Familiarization is to draw near to supreme accomplishment. It resembles considering the route to a city [before a journey]. Proximate practice is to approach the actual practice, resembling preparation for the journey on that route. Practice is to have actually begun the special activity which will yield a particular result, resembling setting out on the route to the city. Great practice is to attain the result without impediment. This resembles entering the gate of the city. (*Encyclopedia*, Volume 3, page 432)

Kongtrul defines the scope of the practice within this lineage and describes its origins:

> The process of purification is based on the awakened experience of body, speech, and mind — the three vajras which are inseparable from the individual, since they are continually present during the basis, path, and result of meditation practice. What must be purified are the obscurations produced by transient, mistaken fixation on the ordinary experience of body, speech, and mind, including the habitual patterns associated with the four circumstances [waking life, dream, deep sleep, and sexual intercourse]. Purification is effected by the branches of familiarization — withdrawal of the senses and mental stability; the branches of practice — vitality control and retention; and the branches of great practice — recollection and meditative absorption. The result of this purification for the most astute and diligent is the actualization of the three expressions of enlightenment [physical, verbal, and mental] during this very lifetime.

> The meditation instructions [for this practice] were directly bestowed by the mother of the buddhas, Vajra Yogini, as her heart's essence, to the great accomplished master Orgyenpa Rinchenpal. [Before meeting her,] this master had thoroughly trained in both the discourses and tantras of the Buddha.... He journeyed to the western region of Oddiyana by overpowering all impediments and frightening magical appearances through his powerful gaze and his conduct which conformed to tantric discipline. He received the blessing of four dakinis in the four directions of the central region of Dumatala and proceeded to the town of Kawoka, following the prophetic advice of a beautiful woman who was an incarnation [of an enlightened being]. There Vajra Yogini first presented herself to him in the guise of a prostitute: the food, drink, and physical pleasure she gave him unbound all the knots in his inner channels. Then in the midst of prodigious signs such as sounds and an earthquake, she revealed her real form as Vajra Queen and bestowed this complete cycle of instruction to him. In addition, the four dakinis he had met previously and Lion-Faced Dakini each gave him some instructions. He attained stability on the level of great accomplishment. (*Encyclopedia*, Volume 1, pages 552-53)

Orgyen Rinchenpal (1230-1309) had been a disciple of the second Karmapa. He is remembered particularly as the principal master of the third Karmapa, Rangjung Dorjay, who initiated the spread of the Intensive Practice Instruction Lineage within the Oral Instruction Lineage of the Karmapas, as Kongtrul explains:

> The second buddha, the omniscient spontaneously appearing lord of spiritual life [Rangjung Dorjay], received all the meditation instructions from the great accomplished one [Orgyenpa]. He unravelled the knots in the vajra words [of the instructions] and illuminated this excellent path which contains vital instructions superior to all others. The Karmapas in their successive incarnations ([the fourth Karmapa,] Lord Rolpay Dorjay, and the rest) and their lineage of disciples spread these instructions far and wide. (*ibid*, Volume 1, page 554)

The Retreat Program for the Vajra Yoga Instruction Lineage Meditations

To complete the second year of the retreat, six months are spent meditating on the phases of creation and completion of the glorious Wheel of Time. During the two weeks devoted to the preliminary practices which cultivate merit and awareness and effect purification, the great empowerment [called] Entering as a Child is given over two days — the first for the preparation, the second for the actual empowerment. After the reading transmission for all the necessary practice texts used for [visualizing] the configuration of the deities and instruction in the intensive practice have been given, [meditation on] the nine deities [in the configuration of Wheel of Time] is done for two and a half months. During that period, the *hamcha* mantra should be recited one million times and the meditations of burning, pressure, descent, merging, the descent of wisdom, etc., should each be done to the extent you are able. These meditations are completed by three days of offering practice and fire rituals.

The three isolations are then meditated upon for three weeks according to the stages described in the manual of the phase of completion, *Meaningful to Behold*. Then the higher supreme empowerments are bestowed. Once the instructions for withdrawal of the senses are taught and the sacred blessing is imparted, [the stages of] withdrawal of the senses and mental stability are meditated upon for two months. As the instructions are given for each of the four [subsequent] stages — vitality control, retention, recollection, and meditative absorption — meditation is done on each for ten days. The auxiliary practices, such as transference of consciousness, must be included as supplementary meditations. If there is a need and an important reason for doing so, the empowerments of vajra master, chief, and great chief will be given during [the period devoted to meditations on] recollection or meditative absorption. There is no need to accompany these [empowerments] with many additional instructions.

THE ANCIENT INSTRUCTION LINEAGE

The Origin of the Lineage

The last year of the retreat is spent meditating on instructions from the Ancient Instruction Lineage. Guru Rinpochay, the great master from Oddiyana in the northwest of the Indian subcontinent, is the central pillar of this lineage. His arrival in the Himalayan region in the ninth century signalled the successful beginning of tantric Buddhist practice there. Guru Rinpochay's continuing pervasive influence exceeded the limits of the Ancient Instruction Lineage, however; Kongtrul considered this master to be the towering central figure responsible for the flourishing of all Buddhist practice in the Himalayas. In *The Ritual of Offering to the Spiritual Masters of the Eight Great Practice Lineages,* Kongtrul places Guru Rinpochay at the center of the configuration of spiritual masters. In this retreat manual as well, he tells his retreatants:

> [Two points, however,] form the common basis [of all practices done here]. First, we should all consider ourselves yogis of the highest level of mantra. Second, all Tibetans in general and particularly those who are followers of the Oral Instruction Lineage and the Ancient Instruction Lineage place their deepest confidence for this life and the next in the second buddha, the sole refuge of beings in these dark times, the great master from Oddiyana [Guru Rinpochay].

One of the distinguishing features of tantra is a tremendous diversity in its methods of practice. This is true for the range of meditations offered by the eight practice lineages and nowhere more so than within the Ancient Instruction Lineage, which contains both the original canonical teachings and the more modern treasure teachings.

On the subject of the original transmissions which are united in the Ancient Instruction Lineage, Kongtrul states:

> According to Rongzom Pandit, there were seven transmissions of the Vajra Way of Secret Mantra [within the Ancient Instruction Lineage]: [one each] from the master Padmakara, from Namkay Nyingpo, from Shanting Garbha (who is said to have participated in the consecration of the temples at Samyay and from whom most of the teachings on Destroyer of the Lord of Death originated), from Berotsana, two from Vimalamitra, and [one] from the great Noob [Sang-gyay Yeshay]. (*Encyclopedia,* Volume 1, page 516)

Of the six masters named here, Padmakara ("Lotus-Born," i.e., Guru Rinpochay), Shanting Garbha, and Vimalamitra were Indian masters who came to Tibet; Namkay Nyingpo, Berotsana, and Noob Sang-gyay Yeshay were Tibetans who journeyed to India. Kongtrul first describes Guru Rinpochay's contributions to the streams of transmission that comprise this lineage:

> The great leader who brought the new dawn of the Buddha's teachings to the dark land of the Himalayas was the bodhisattva Gentle Melody [Manjugosha] incarnate, King Trisong Dé'u Tsen. Due to this [king's] exceptional perspicacity and boundless kindness, the protector of beings Buddha Boundless Light, incarnate as the vajra master [Guru Rinpochay], appeared in Tibet. This crowning jewel of all accomplished masters, the second buddha known by eight names including Padmakara, was perceived by his ordinary disciples as teaching only *The Garland of Instructions Concerning the Philosophical View* at [the monastery of] Samyay. To his special disciples with a fortunate connection [to the tantric teachings] (including the five friends — the king and his subjects), [he appeared] mainly at the five great practice places that represent the body, speech, mind, qualities, and activity of enlightenment. At these and all other sacred areas he bestowed an inconceivable number of instructions that mature and liberate [persons on the spiritual path]. [His teachings] included an immeasurable number of practice texts with supplementary activity rituals related to the meditations of the peaceful and wrathful deities of the eight configurations and the cycle of instructions concerning the peaceful and wrathful forms of the spiritual master, which represent the unified inner essence of all the spiritual instructions of radiant Great Perfection....
>
> At Chimpu, Yerpa, and Chuwori, he founded three large monastic meditation centers. He also travelled throughout Ü (Central Tibet), Tsang (Western Tibet), and Kham (Eastern Tibet) through the uninhibited play of his miraculous powers. There is no area of Tibetan soil larger than a horse's hoof that was not touched by his feet. He consecrated all isolated mountainous regions as places of meditation practice. Through his bestowal of instructions to those persons with a fortunate connection to tantra, innumerable accomplished masters appeared. These included the twenty-five accomplished masters of Chimpu, the fifty-five realized ones of Yang Dzong, the hundred and eight persons in both Yerpa and Chuwori who accomplished the body of light, the

> thirty mantra practitioners of Shel Drak, and the twenty-five *dakinis* whose bodies dissolved into the radiant form of awakening. (*ibid*, Volume 1, pages 509-10)

Guru Rinpochay's arrival in Tibet signalled the beginning of an extraordinarily productive period of spiritual ferment in the whole region. As Kongtrul states in *An Impartial History of the Sources of Spiritual Instruction*:

> Of the one hundred scholars who came to Tibet [at that time], the three principal ones were the two great masters who had attained an indestructible body — the great master Tsokyay Dorjay ["Lake-Born Vajra"] from Oddiyana [i.e., Guru Rinpochay] and Vimalamitra from Kashmir — and the very erudite, precious master Bodhisattva [also known as Shantirakshita] from Zahor. A number of translators who were emanations [of bodhisattvas], including the great translator Berotsana [and his colleagues] Kawa Paltsek, Chokro Lu'i Gyaltsen, and Shang Yeshay Day, translated all the most renowned teachings of the Buddha and the treatises of enlightened masters' commentaries existing in India. The great [master from] Oddiyana and others drew many extremely profound secret tantras that were not commonly known to exist in India from the secret treasuries of the dakinis [and brought them to Tibet]. Tibet thus became a place of merit. (page 4a)

The instructions given and the translations completed at that time became the basis for the canon of the Ancient Instruction Lineage and are known as the Original Translations. The transmission of this collection has been passed down in an unbroken series of masters since the time of Guru Rinpochay. This, however, constitutes only a fraction of Guru Rinpochay's legacy to tantric Buddhists. Kongtrul explains:

> The master saw that there was neither a suitable environment nor the need for most of his instructions at that time. Considering the infinite numbers of beings in the future, he concealed his teachings in a million places that are named (for example, the five great treasure sources — one in the center and one in each of the four directions) and innumerable ones without names. He secured these treasures with seven seals. (*ibid*, page 4b)

The transmission of the treasures was to become a lasting source of renewal of Guru Rinpochay's spiritual influence in the Himalayas. Among his numerous disciples it was one many consider to be the foremost, Yeshay Tsogyal, who was principally responsible for the treasures. Kongtrul briefly describes her work in *The History of the Source of the Profound Treasures and the Treasure Revealers*:

> In general, Guru Rinpochay himself concealed in India, Nepal, and Tibet an infinite number of treasures — instructions, riches, medicinal essences, statues, consecrated objects, etc. — in consideration of the needs of future disciples and the prolongation of the doctrine. Here in the Himalayan region he gave general spiritual instructions that reflected his skill in training his disciples in whatever way was appropriate to them. In particular he taught an infinite number of profound instructions and activity rituals connected to the transmissions of the tantras of the three yogas.
>
> All these teachings were collected by the queen of secrets, the powerful woman of the realm of totality, Yeshay Tsogyal, through her perfect memory. She recorded them on yellow parchment in the symbolic scripts of the five classes of dakinis and secured them in various treasure containers with an indestructible seal. These were concealed and entrusted to the treasure guardians by Guru Rinpochay and her alone or together with the king and the closest disciples of the master. In particular, after Guru Rinpochay had left Tibet for [the realm of] Tail-Fan Island, Yeshay Tsogyal, who lived for more than one hundred years, concealed and secured the sites of an inconceivable number of treasures throughout upper, lower, and central Tibet. (pages 34b-35a)

Some of Guru Rinpochay's other close disciples also concealed treasures. Kongtrul here is referring to treasures concealed under the earth, but treasures have also been revealed in other locations — in visions, in the mind, from memory, etc. Those who reveal them were members of the circle of Guru Rinpochay's disciples in a previous life. As Kongtrul again explains:

> Those who are known as the one hundred major and the one thousand minor treasure revealers are actual reincarnations or emanations of those who were destined to be brought to spiritual maturity within the indestructible configurations of deities by the great [master from] Oddiyana.... The treasures [they reveal] consist of whatever is appropriate to help beings at a particular time — spiritual instructions, riches, consecrated objects, medicine, areas of sacred ground, etc. This activity will continue until the appearance of the doctrine of [the next Buddha,] Loving-Kindness. (*An Impartial History*, pages 4b-5a)

The Source of the Meditations of this Stage of the Retreat

There are three major meditations practiced during this stage of the retreat: the creation phase meditations of Vajrasattva and Yangdak Heruka, and the completion phase meditations of Great Perfection.

The Vajrasattva meditation is a treasure text revealed by Orgyen Terdak Lingpa (also known as Gyurmay Dorjay) (1646-1714). Kongtrul mentions that this practice unites both the canonical and treasure transmissions of the Ancient Instruction Lineage.

The meditation of Yangdak Heruka finds its origins in the canon as Kongtrul explains in *The Encyclopedia of Buddhism*:

> Namkay Nyingpo travelled to India and received the entire cycle of Yangdak Heruka practices from the master Humkara. His body became the expression of non-dual wisdom. The lineage of practice originating with him, the So tradition of instructions for Yangdak Heruka, has reached the present day. (Volume 1, page 514)

Kongtrul relates both practices to Terdak Lingpa, the original compiler of the canon. Because many of the texts used during the retreat originate with this master or members of his family, it seems appropriate to include here Kongtrul's testimonial to this master from *The History of the Source of the Profound Treasures and the Treasure Revealers*:

> Terdak Lingpa and the great excellent gathering [of persons around him] were responsible for a full proliferation of the practice and explanation of spiritual instructions, and of enlightened activity. Since their time until today it would seem that every creditable stream of instruction within the canonical or treasure teachings of the Original School of Translation passed through this group.... Not only did this outstanding holy person extend his great kindness personally or through his lineage to the whole doctrine of Original and Later Schools, he also nourished the lesser streams of instruction — the Jonang, Shangpa, Pacification of Suffering, Severance, and others — through his own effort or through his encouragement to others. Most particularly, at the time when the practice and explanation lineages of the original Ancient Instruction Lineage were about to disappear like a tiny stream in winter, he courageously and energetically sought [the teachings that existed] and wrote many new treatises on the configurations of practice and other subjects.... He repaired the foundations of the supreme

> original tradition's doctrine through elucidation, practice, and enlightened activity....
>
> His collected works extend to thirteen volumes of Buddhist treatises. I myself have unconditional faith in this work and have not forgotten his kindness. I have energetically sought and received the entire reading transmission of the Mindrol Ling tradition and have done as much as I can to perform the intensive practice of the New Treasures and to teach them. By initiating [in the retreat center] the regular practices of Yangdak Heruka of the So tradition and that of Vajrasattva and other practices from Terdak Lingpa's own treasures, I have accomplished a little activity for the doctrine of this tradition. I aspire to continue to do so for as long as I live. (pages 73b-74a)

The third practice of this stage of the retreat is the Great Perfection meditation of the Secret Vital Essence, a blend of the "mother and child" instructions of the Heart-Essence of Vimalamitra. The "mother" instructions originate with Vimalamitra's teaching in Tibet; the "child" instructions are those Longchenpa discovered as a treasure within his own mind, called *The Innermost Essence of the Spiritual Master*. Kongtrul describes the origins of this transmission in *The Encyclopedia of Buddhism*:

> The crowning jewel of five hundred scholars, Master Vimalamitra, who attained an indestructible rainbow-like body, [also] came to Tibet. He bestowed the teachings concerning the category of instructions of Great Perfection to Nyang Ben Tingdzin Zangpo, who possessed prescience. [Once he had practiced these instructions,] Nyang Ben's [physical form] dissolved into light.... The oral transmission [of the teachings] was passed from Nyang Ben to Bay Lodrö Wangchuk; the written transmission was gathered [and hidden] as a treasure, later revealed by Dangma Lhun-gyal. This master also received the oral transmission and bestowed all of these instructions to Chetsun Sengay Wangchuk who became liberated into a body of light. These instructions, which became known as the Heart-Essence of Vimalamitra, were passed from Chetsun to Gyalwa Shangton and down through a series of masters....
>
> [The instructions eventually reached] the omniscient Drimay Özer [Longchenpa]. The inspiration which overflowed into this master's mind from the expanse of the Buddha Ever-Excellent's [Samantabhadra's] enlightened awareness produced *The Innermost Essence of the Spiritual*

> *Master, The Profound Inner Essence, The Innermost Essence of the Dakinis, The Seven Treasuries*, the root text and commentary to *Kindly Bent to Ease Us*, and other works. [This master's instruction] bore many exceptional disciples who upheld this lineage. In brief, the doctrine of the Secret Vital Essence which transforms the solid composite form of the body into a body of light was suffused by this master's influence and disseminated by him. He is known as Longchen Rabjam Zangpo, a veritable second Garab Dorjay [the first member of the lineage of Great Perfection]. (Volume 1, page 512)

This lineage also provided the inspiration for three other treasure teachings of Great Perfection: the Heart-Essence of the Karmapa, revealed by the third Karmapa, Rangjung Dorjay, after he had a vision of Vimalamitra who appeared and dissolved into his forehead; the Heart-Essence of Longchenpa, revealed by Jikmay Lingpa (1729-1798) after he had three visions of Longchenpa; and the Profound Vital Essence of Vimalamitra, a series of instructions recalled by Jamyang Kyentsay Wangpo at the age of twenty-four. The catalyst for the recollection was a vision he had of Chetsun Sengay Wangchuk.

The Treasury of Rediscovered Teachings

One of the five treasuries that Jamgon Kongtrul composed or compiled during his lifetime was a collection of treasure texts called *The Treasury of Rediscovered Teachings*. The modern edition of this collection stretches to sixty large volumes. The conferral of the empowerments and reading transmissions of these teachings is a daunting task both for the master and for the disciples. In recent years, both His Holiness Dujom Rinpochay and Dilgo Kyentsay Rinpochay bestowed this collection to many people on a number of occasions during their lifetimes.

Within the Oral Instruction Lineage of the Karmapas, Jamgon Kongtrul bestowed the transmission of this collection to the fifteenth Karmapa who in turn passed it on to his son, Kyentsay Özer, a reincarnation of Jamgon Kongtrul. Although the sixteenth Karmapa had received this collection, he did not live to pass it on to the new generation of incarnate masters of his tradition. He advised them to request the empowerments and reading transmissions of this collection from another incarnation of Jamgon Kongtrul, Kalu Rinpochay. Accordingly, Kalu Rinpochay bestowed this collection in 1983 to a large gathering headed by the incarnate masters of the Oral Instruction Lineage of the Karmapas.

In *The Encyclopedia of Buddhism*, Kongtrul comments on the future of the treasure practices:

> The spiritual heirs to these [treasure] instructions and their disciples who maintain their lineages will uphold the instructions for spiritual life during the last stages of these adverse times. Even where the doctrines of monastic discipline and the discourses of the Buddha disappear, the doctrine of the Vajra Way of Secret Mantra will not fade even slightly. Instead, it will grow and flourish, providing a continual source of far-reaching enlightened activity that liberates all, even those who are disinclined to spiritual life. (Volume 1, page 516)

The Retreat Program for the Ancient Instruction Lineage Meditations

At the beginning of the third year, the empowerments and the [combined] reading transmissions and instructions must be given for the Heart Practice of Vajrasattva and [the meditation on] the nine semicircles of Yangdak Heruka in the So tradition. [During the subsequent practices,] the six-syllable heart [mantra] of Vajrasattva must be recited six hundred thousand times; the hundred-syllable mantra, one hundred thousand times; and the *rulu* mantra of Yangdak Heruka, eight hundred thousand times. Each of these two practices should be completed by a great practice session, including the continual recitation of mantras, for seven full days and one morning. If that is not done, an offering practice to the configuration of deities should be done for three days for each meditation. To complete the practice, the burning and pouring [fire ritual] to produce a pacifying effect should be done for two days for each meditation. All these stages of the intensive meditation practice of the peaceful and wrathful forms of Vajrasattva are to be finished within a three-month period.[32]

---

[32] Tantric deities are grouped into classes (rig, *rigs*) according to the aspect of enlightened awareness they represent. Both Vajrasattva and Yangdak Heruka belong to the vajra class of deities; the former is a peaceful form, the latter wrathful.

Then the wish-fulfilling jewel intricate empowerment of Great Perfection practice, *The Innermost Essence of the Spiritual Master*, is bestowed. Detailed instruction in the visualizations [of the meditations], beginning with the preliminary practices, is then given in stages according to the oral instructions of Drimay Özer [Longchenpa].

[First, reflection and meditation on the seven mental trainings] must be completed in twenty-seven days. To begin with, impermanence, immediate and long-term happiness, life's unpredictability, the meaninglessness of past acts, the Buddha's qualities, and the profound instructions of the spiritual master are all reflected upon for three days each. The three aspects of the last of the seven mental trainings [non-discursiveness] — bliss, clarity, and non-discursiveness [in pure being] — are each meditated upon for three days. Then, the common [methods of] cultivating merit and awareness and effecting purification — taking refuge, [reciting] the hundred-syllable mantra, [offering] the universe in a symbolic form, and union with the mind of the spiritual master — are practiced for seven days each, a total of twenty-eight days. [During this time,] the first half of the meditation session should be devoted to the common recitation and meditation practices and the last half to the special recitations and meditations. In this way, the common and special practices are performed together.

Following this, the desire-free energy wind is learned: the color, shape, number, exhalation and inhalation, and blue vase [breathing are all meditated upon] for three days each.[33]

---

[33] Energy wind (loong, *rlung*) is most commonly known in the West by the Chinese word "chi," as in tai-chi exercises. In general, a person's mental and physical state depends upon the circulation of numerous energy winds within the body. Imbalances or blocks in the circulation of these energy winds lead to physical and mental illnesses; proper circulation results in physical well-being and mental good cheer. The object of most tantric meditations on the energy winds is not therapeutic but to intensify and focus the mind's energy.

Vase breathing (boompa chen, *bum pa can*) is a method of breath retention. "Blue vase breathing" (boompa chen ngonpo, *bum pa can sngon po*) is a literal translation of the text: I suspect a mistake since I have found no reference to this in the lengthy commentary Kongtrul wrote on the practice.

Including the five days spent on learning the desire-free vital essence,[34] [the period spent on these meditations is] twenty days. Three days are then spent meditating on each of the five Ah's-Without-Origination, each [connected] to one of the five elements (a total of fifteen days). From the beginning of the seven mental trainings until this point, these preliminary practices take three months.

Once the unelaborate empowerment is given, [the practice of] Cutting Through the Solidity of Clinging [Trek Chö, *khregs chod*] is meditated upon for three months. To begin with, one month is spent training [in all its preliminary practices]. Five days are spent performing the physical [preliminary practice of] vajra posture. The four stages of the verbal [preliminary practice] — sealing, developing strength, producing force, and entering the path — are practiced for five days each. Five days are also spent [on the mental preliminary practice]: examining the three aspects of mental activity — [its point of] origin, [the location of its actual] presence, and [the place to which it] passes away.

Beginning with the practice of resting in a natural state, two months are spent on the main practice [of Cutting Through the Solidity of Clinging]. During that time, instructions which introduce the nature of mind, including A Rain of Blessing, must be given. You should meditate assiduously.

Then Direct Vision [Tögal, *thod rgal*] [is meditated upon] for three months. To begin with, seven days are spent meditating on distinguishing cyclic existence from perfect peace, after which the empowerments of extreme simplicity and total simplicity are bestowed. After resting in whatever natural state is appropriate, luminosity is learned in connection with physical postures, styles of gazing, etc.

---

[34] Vital essence (tig lay, *thig le*) is, as the name implies, the substance that represents the core of our psycho-physical being; it is sometimes translated as "drop." "Desire-free vital esence" (chak dral tig lay, *chags bral thig le*) is clearly written in this text, although Kongtrul's commentary designates this stage of the practice "passionate vital essence" (chak chen, *chags can*).

Once the door to the clear nature of phenomena is seen, the instructions and visualizations for those of moderate and average capabilities are given together. The visualization for transference of consciousness is practiced whenever appropriate.

The four crucial points of the cycle of pure being that produce the continual stream of yoga are explained from the beginning of the practice of Cutting Through the Solidity of Clinging and should be practiced. During that practice (or at any other time, before or after, that is convenient) the meditation and mantra recitation practice of the Three Sources of Wish-Fulfillment — the spiritual master, the meditation deity, and the dakini — [should be performed]. During the practice of Direct Vision, the outer, inner, secret, and very secret practices of the spiritual master according to *Wish-Fulfilling Ambrosia: The Essential Instructions of Luminosity* and [meditations from] the great Chetsun's *Profound Vital Essence of Vimalamitra* should be practiced as you are able.

ADDITIONAL PRACTICES PERFORMED DURING THE RETREAT

Whenever convenient during spare time, the complete reading transmission for all [the following texts] should be given: the three volumes of Shangpa instructions, the two volumes concerning the protector, the one volume on the Six Branches of Application, and the one volume on *The Innermost Essence of the Spiritual Master*.

At the end of the first year, the meditation of the Integrated Practice of the Four Deities should be done for one week. Similarly, the torma ritual called *A Treasure Vault of Enlightened Activity* [is performed] at the end of the second year and the mantra recitation of the Swift-Acting Fully Awakened Protector (based on the activity ritual of the outer practice of the New Treasures) at the end of the third.

For the first meditation, the Integrated Practice of the Four Deities, the empowerment-blessing and the instruction must be given. For the second, [you must receive] the torma empowerments and combined reading transmission and instruction for the practices of Dispelling All Obstacles, the Inseparability of the Spiritual Master and the Protector, the Elimination of Obscurations, and the Descent of the Essence. For the third [practice], the torma empowerment-blessing and the reading transmission [must be bestowed].

These recitation practices are done in conjunction with the year-end practice of torma offering [to Six-Armed Protector]. The two weeks [devoted to these practices] each year, counted together, equal forty-two days. These must be counted within the three fortnights [of the retreat].

As the time for opening the retreat approaches, the virtuous [practice] to complete [the retreat] is the mantra recitation and offering practice of the noble woman, Wish-Fulfilling Wheel (White Tara), performed for one week. This practice and the longevity practices of Niguma and Sukasiddhi done previously are all counted as being performed during the extra lunar month that is sure to occur during any three-year period.[35]

EXIT FROM THE RETREAT

When the three-year, three-fortnight period is finished, an astrologically auspicious and virtuous date should be chosen [for the exit]. On that morning, a fragrant smoke offering of thanksgiving to the gods should be made and *The Three-Part Torma Offering* ceremony performed. Once the list of the retreatants is removed, you may meet those who have a pure relationship to tantric Buddhism. [During this first day,] you should only go outside to circumambulate the retreat center. On the following day, for example, you should go to the main monastery, make offerings of the universe in a symbolic form at the upper and lower temples

---

[35] The lunar calendar has a maximum of 360 days in a year. To allow it to correspond to the solar calendar, an additional month is added every few years to the Tibetan calendar. For example, 1989 and 1991 were both years of thirteen months.

there, and then visit the spiritual brothers of our refuge and protector [Tai Situpa].

Before much time elapses, you should enter retreat again. [This time,] you should meditate on the Buddha of Complete Awareness [Maha Vairochana] for six months, followed by ten days of fire rituals to complete the practice. Three months should be spent meditating on Unshakable Buddha [Akshobya], along with burning and pouring fire rituals at the completion. [Finally,] one month should be passed performing the ritual of the Buddha of Boundless Light from the Sky Treasures.[36] All of these practices must be done faithfully in your room in this retreat center.

---

[36] The Sky Treasures (Namchö, *gnam chos*) originate with Mingyur Dorjay, a discoverer of treasure texts through visions (from the age of twelve) and within his mind (from the age of sixteen). Karma Chakmay, one of his teachers, would compose meditations, instructions, and rituals based on these teachings. Mingyur Dorjay lived just twenty-four years but the treasure texts he discovered were very numerous and continue to be of great importance.

2. The Daily Schedule

BACKGROUND INFORMATION

The meditations mentioned above in the three-year, three-fortnight program fit into a daily program of four periods of meditation. Kongtrul does not provide details of the length of each session — two and a half to three hours would seem likely, as is common in many modern retreats. The morning and afternoon group sessions would be somewhat shorter, perhaps lasting one and a half hours each.

The practices described in this section fall within the following categories:

1. The yoga of sleep or waking from sleep. The former is mentioned but not described. The latter consists of five stages: clearing away stagnant energy wind, resting the mind, engendering the sacred dignity of complete identification with the meditation deity, tasting consecrated nectar, and blessing the voice. Just as our daily routine begins with personal morning rituals of washing, choice of clothing, eating, preparation for the day's activities, etc., so the meditator's day begins with these stages of practice. All of these practices aim at uplifting the meditator's experience of embodiment and enworldment.

The third of these stages, engendering the sacred dignity of complete identification with the meditation deity, has often been translated as "vajra pride," from the Tibetan expression meaning divine pride or pride of the deity. While the meditator might conceive of himself or herself as many different meditation deities in the course of a day, this pride or sacred dignity born of complete immersion within a deity's form and world would ideally remain constant. It is this which Kongtrul is encouraging his retreatants to maintain even during sleep when he tells them, "You should not acquiesce to the force of habit of your ordinary sense of self during sleep. It should be transformed into the spiritual path through techniques of the yoga of sleep...."

2. *Reaffirmation of vows.* Vows and commitments related to the three Buddhist disciplines are reaffirmed on numerous occasions throughout the day, particularly during the main part of the morning group session. Prayers relating to these commitments are also recited at the beginning of the second session and after the last.

3. *Prayers to Guru Rinpochay.* Prayers accompanied by meditation on Guru Rinpochay are recited throughout the day. These are mainly taken from a collection called *The Seven Prayers.* These prayers were spoken by Guru Rinpochay when five of his main disciples assembled and requested him to compose prayers according to their needs. One was given to them collectively and one each individually. The seventh prayer is *The Prayer for the Spontaneous Fulfillment of Wishes,* given to one of the five on a later occasion. Kongtrul also includes *The Prayer to Dispel Obstacles on the Path* in the day's program. This treasure text was retrieved by Chok-gyur Daychen Lingpa during the nineteenth century and has become a well-loved prayer since that time.

4. *Meditations from the Secret Vital Essence.* In the vicinity of Kongtrul's retreat, Chok-gyur Daychen Lingpa retrieved a treasure text containing three meditations. This cycle of practices is called the Secret Vital Essence and consists of meditations on Vajrasattva, Yangdak Heruka, and Vajra Dagger. All three meditations were done by the retreatants daily — during the first and third sessions and after the last, respectively.

5. *Offerings to spirits or prevention of harmful influences.* Buddhism recognizes many spirits that are said to invisibly fill the world around us. These are usually not mentioned as objects of fear but as beings who might be aided by a compassionate meditator. Kongtrul has his retreatants feed the starving spirits water tormas in the morning and portions of food before and after the noon meal. The last part of the afternoon group session is dedicated to meditations, mantras, and prayers aimed at preventing harm caused by spirits whose influence is wholly detrimental to spiritual life. The fourth meditation session begins with an offering of burnt food to the beings who are suspended

within the intermediate state between death and rebirth. Their disorientation and fear is said to be assuaged by food which they can only receive in the form of smells; thus their name, "smell-eaters." The day ends with an offering of one's body to the sources of refuge and to all beings. Within the context of this practice, the beings mentioned often include spirits, gods, and demons who are pacified by the offerings.

6. Offerings to the protectors. The main part of the afternoon group session consists of meditations on, and offerings to, the protectors of Buddhism. These are usually bodhisattvas or emanations of bodhisattvas who have promised to protect all those who follow the Buddha's ways of spiritual development. Their influence is invoked so that their enlightened activity will prevent obstacles for the retreat community. Although Tara is not a protector, her activity is such that the recitation of the praises to Green Tara done during the morning group session also falls into this category.

7. Longevity practices. Meditations to increase the well-being of the meditator, called longevity practices, are performed during the first meditation session of the day. *The Prayer to Prevent Untimely Death* and a long-life prayer for Kongtrul recited at the end of the afternoon group session can also be considered longevity practices.

8. Dedication of merit. Prayers to dedicate the effects of one's actions to the welfare of all beings are recited at the completion of any meditation. Kongtrul makes particular note of the prayers recited for the benefit of the patron who provided the noon meal and the prayers of dedication to be done at the end of the afternoon group session.

9. The yoga of food. On the subject of food, Kongtrul mentions only a noon meal but one strongly suspects that the morning and afternoon group sessions were used as such sessions are in Buddhist monasteries: as time for prayers punctuated by the serving of simple meals. The noon meal was eaten as a vajra feast according to instructions from a treasure text which begins:

> ...those who claim, "I am a tantric practitioner"
> But eat food without [relying on the methods of] creation
> and completion meditations
> Are no different from dogs and pigs enjoying their meals.

The point here, as with most of the above practices, is to bring the "sacred dignity" of meditation to the table as to any facet of daily life.

What is conspicuous by its absence from the program is any time allotted to study. Kongtrul intended that his retreat be conducted exactly as he planned; this did not include any extraneous study. As he remarks later on in this text,

> Those persons who are unfamiliar with Buddhism may study, on entering the retreat, those texts of the program mentioned above as being indispensable and specifically those textbooks explaining the three disciplines. Apart from those few books, no study, research, or examination of any texts concerning the major or minor subjects of the study of Buddhism is permitted under any circumstances. Study, reflection, and mental training are ordinarily considered vital to our spiritual lives. However, when the practice of meditation is our major concern, the many sources of discursive thought intrinsic to study act as obstacles to our development of meditative experience. Because one session of valid meditation practice is far more valuable than an entire lifetime devoted to study and reflection, we here are satisfied with wholehearted meditation practice.

THE SEVERANCE INSTRUCTION LINEAGE

Within the dense forest of daily meditations that supplement the main practices of the retreat, Kongtrul mentions one by stating simply, "the meditation of offering one's body to the sources of refuge and to all beings." This meditation is central to the Severance Instruction Lineage, borne of the enlightened genius of a Tibetan woman, Ma Chik Labdron (1031-1129).

Ma Chik was recognized as a child prodigy and completed a thorough religious education early in her life. She received instructions in one form of Severance, "the male transmission," from Kyo Sonam Lama who in turn had received them from Dampa Sang-gyay, an Indian yogi who journeyed to Tibet five times during his extremely long life.[37] His main instructions became known as the Pacification of Suffering Instruction Lineage. Because Dampa Sang-gyay was one of Ma Chik's principal masters and their lineages became intricately connected, Kongtrul considered the Pacification of Suffering Instruction Lineage and the Severance Instruction

---

[37] Dampa Sang-gyay is often called Pa-dampa Sang-gyay. *Pa,* meaning "father" in Tibetan, was added to his name because Ma Chik's children called him father. Their father, Töpa Bhadra, was also a dark-skinned Indian yogi. Dampa Sang-gyay was also called Dharma Bodhi, the name by which he was known when he and Milarepa met. See *The Hundred Thousand Songs of Milarepa,* Volume 2, Chapter 33.

Lineage together as one of the eight practice lineages.

The "female transmission" of Severance was entirely Ma Chik's own, as Kongtrul explains in *An Impartial History of the Sources of Spiritual Instruction*:

> Ma Chik Labdron was an incarnation of the Great Mother [a name for the female buddha Prajna-Paramita ("Perfection of Appreciative Discernment")]. Ultimately she herself was none other than this vajra queen who is the mother of all buddhas, but on the relative level of ordinary appearances, she demonstrated the way of attaining accomplishment by giving birth to the realization of the perfection of appreciative discernment.[38] The instructions of Severance she spread that sprang from the vitality [of her realization] became known as the female transmission of Severance. (pages 13a-b)

The name "Severance" is simply a device to avoid the longer name of the instruction lineage: The Domain of Severing the Demons [of Self-Attachment]. Even Ma Chik was aware of the ease with which such a name can be misunderstood: she would remind her disciples that a demon is not something that looms large, dark, and threatening in the night. The real demon that plagues us, she would explain, is our own self-centeredness which keeps us imprisoned within the bounds of life in cyclic existence. As Kongtrul explains in *The Encyclopedia of Buddhism*:

> Just as one must know the location of the ground where one will cut wood, the place to sever the demons of self-centered discursive thoughts is the [ground of] the perfection of appreciative discernment. (Volume 1, page 543)

Besides being an incomparable meditation master, Ma Chik Labdron was a mother and a poet. Her many children, both boys and girls, carried on her tradition of meditation. They and many of her spiritual children throughout the centuries have produced beautiful poems and songs following her example. Neither she nor her offspring were institution builders, yet as Kongtrul remarks:

> The enlightened activity of the profound practices of the Severance Instruction Lineage has been astonishing: it has pervaded the entire Himalayan region, far and wide. [Since its inception] until today, the meditations of Severance have

[38] Appreciative discernment (prajna; shey-rab, *shes rab*), a central term in Great Way Buddhism, is often translated as "wisdom," "awareness," and "discriminating awareness."

> been part of the personal practice of every impartial spiritual guide [of this region]. (*ibid*, Volume 1, page 546)

Ma Chik is a refreshing, lively presence among the typical men-in-hats style preferred by the artists of most Tibetan lineages. She is depicted in paintings as she is visualized in Severance meditations: dancing naked. The feeling-tone is not simply sexual: her presence conveys free and awakened feminine well-being, lucent insight, and unbounded delight. She was also a skilful teacher: the record of answers she gave orally to disciples' questions reveal a relaxed and eloquent speaker, both comfortable and generous with words.

Those who practice Ma Chik's Severance meditations continue to be nourished by her influence and occasionally inspired by the presence of her reincarnations. Of all the lineages of her practice, Kongtrul considered that of the series of incarnations of Trungpa Rinpochay of Zurmang Monastery to be the best, as he states in *A Concise Manual for the Practice of Severance*:

> Severance is known throughout the schools of the Original and Later Tantras; different traditions of its practice are exceedingly numerous. However I consider this transmission of the Zurmang tradition to be the lineage descending [from Ma Chik]. Because the stream of its plentiful profound instructions has not diminished... and the blessing of its instructions has not been interrupted, it is superior to all other [transmissions of the Severance practices]. (pages 1b-2a)

THE ORDER OF THE YOGA OF THE FOUR DAILY MEDITATION SESSIONS THAT MUST BE DONE FAITHFULLY

During each of the four [stages of the retreat] — the preliminary practices, the meditations from the Shangpa Instruction Lineage, of the Six Branches of Application, and on Great Perfection — the yoga of the four daily meditation sessions determines the experience of meditation and the post-meditative state of mind (i.e., the basic attentiveness maintained during the meditations-in-action of the four circumstances — waking consciousness, sleep, etc.). The instruction manual for each practice provides [the specific details of the meditations to be done during those times]. [Two points, however,] form the common basis [of all practices]. First, we should all consider ourselves yogis of the highest level of mantra. Second, all Tibetans in general and particularly those who are followers of the Oral Instruction Lineage and the Ancient Instruction Lineage place their deepest confidence for this life and the next in the second buddha, the sole refuge of beings of these dark times, the great master from Oddiyana [Guru Rinpochay].

The First Meditation Session

[You begin] the morning with the yoga of waking from sleep in the style appropriate to [the stage of the retreat, be it] creation phase or completion phase meditation. [To begin with,] you clear away stagnant energy wind three times. Assuming a straight posture, you rest without discursive thought for as long as possible in a natural state of mind. Once you have [engendered] the sacred dignity of [complete identification with] your main meditation deity, you taste consecrated nectar: If you have nectar pills, Dharma medicine, or other [blessed substances], you may swallow them. If not, you place close by a skull-cup in which the contents are fermented by these substances, and you renew the consecration of them by extensive or abridged meditations, as appropriate. If you do not do these, you repeat the mantra *om ah hung ho* three times, imagining that [the contents of the skull-cup] are the indivisible union of the nectars of commitment and wisdom.[39] Then you taste them with [the tip of] the ring finger of the left hand.

Following this, you bless your voice by one of two methods. You may develop the potency of the power of mantra recitation according to [the instructions of] the Quintessential Vision of the Spiritual Master, if you know and enjoy doing [the meditation]. Alternatively, you may recite the vowels and syllables [of the Sanskrit alphabet] three or more times in conjunction with the meditation

---

[39] During the consecration of this offering, the nectar produced through the visualization of the meditator is called the nectar of commitment (dam tsik, *dam tshig*); the nectar produced by the blessing of the buddhas is called the nectar of wisdom (yeshay, *ye shes*).

written by Garwang Chökyi Wangchuk.[40]

You then recite the description of the visualization [to be done concurrently with] *The Seven Prayers*[41] written by Minling Terchen. You raise your voice to recite [two] prayers [from this collection:] *The Prayer to the Spiritual Master's Three Forms* and *The Prayer Given to Yeshay Tsogyal.* When you [reach the line] "Arise, Master Lotus-Born!" [in the second prayer], you accompany [your recitation with] hand-drum and bell. Once finished, you [imagine that you] receive empowerment and that [the visualized forms] melt into light and dissolve into you. [These last stages] are repeated whenever the visualized framework is created before the recitation of the prayers from this collection. The combined reading transmission and instruction [for this practice] according to *A Rain of Blessings* by the Buddha's son, Payma Gyurmay Gyatso, must be given as soon as the retreat begins. The lineage of these instructions is unbroken and this visualized framework represents the pith of the enlightened intention of the Heart-Essence of the Awareness Holders, the first of the treasures discovered by Minling Terchen.

Following this, you quickly perform the meditation and mantra recitation of White Tara, Wish-Fulfilling Wheel. When your dreams have been troubled and at other times of need, you recite the mantras and do the meditation of a protective enclosure.[42]

Once [all these practices] have been completed, you begin the principal virtuous practice of that particular stage of the

---

[40] I have been unable to find this practice by this author. I strongly suspect a printing error — in another text Kongtrul includes a short meditation of this type written by Kyungpo Naljor.

[41] It would seem that the visualized framework that Kongtrul is referring to is that contained within the book mentioned below, *A Rain of Blessings*, by the son of Minling Terchen. The subject of this book is meditation on union with the mind of the spiritual master. It specifically provides a visualization of Guru Rinpochay and suggests the recitation of *The Seven Prayers* during the meditation.

[42] The visualization of a protective enclosure (soong kor, *srung 'khor*) to provide security from obstacles and negative influences is a common element in tantric meditations.

retreat, be it the preliminary practices to Great Seal meditation, the visualization of yourself as the deity during the practices of the creation phase of meditation, the doctrine of inner heat during the practices of the completion phase of meditation, or other meditation practices.

As daybreak approaches at the end of the session, you meditate on the yoga of the single form of Vajrasattva from the cycle of the Secret Vital Essence. You recite the hundred-syllable mantra twenty-one times and the *sato* mantra during the round of one *mala* [i.e., 108 times]. Having previously prepared a full ceremonial vase, you recite as many mantras of the vase visualization as you wish, then imagine that you receive empowerment. You may also do a meditation and recitation of mantras for longevity.

At daybreak you perform either a medium-length or a short offering of water tormas. If you take this practice lightly and are careless — arranging the offerings the night before, or allowing the offerings to become dirty, etc. — this ritual will do more harm than good. Therefore, you should conscientiously learn the stages of the visualizations and the practical procedures [of the offering] and then follow them scrupulously.

The Morning Group Session

Immediately after the meditation session finishes, you must assemble in the Great Glorious Temple. To begin with, *The Seven-Line Invocation of Guru Rinpochay*, *The Prayer Given to Namkai Nyingpo* [from *The Seven Prayers*], and *Twenty-one Homages in Praise of Tara* are recited. An abridged form of *The Ladder to Freedom* is then performed, as described at the end of that text. [The ritual includes] the essentials of cultivating merit and awareness: [you recite the section] of "remembering the spiritual master and the Buddha" while maintaining the essential view of certain truth; you acknowledge all the infractions [incurred in your training] during the course of the day by reciting *The Discourse of Three Clusters* and the prayer [that begins], "The master who holds the vajra"; and [you recite the prayers for] the purification and renewal of [the vows for] living in peace, the acceptance of the commitment to develop the mind of awakening, and the commitments of mantra practice.

The Second Meditation Session

At the beginning of the morning meditation session, you recite *The Twenty-five Vows*, changing the words [at the end of the lines of the prayer] to those of a promise not to commit [unvirtuous acts]. [As you recite] you should remain mindful of the words' meanings. You then begin the main practice of virtue according to the stage of the retreat.

The Noon Break

At noon you recite *Remembering the Three Jewels Discourse* before [eating]. From the food that is still clean [i.e., before you begin eating], you take a portion to offer [to the Buddha, etc.] and one to make a *chong-bu*[43] to give to [the spirit] Trokma. The noon meal is eaten according to the yoga of food — you enjoy it as an inner vajra feast, following the directions of [*Offering a Vajra Feast to One's Own Body*], a text that combines a treasure teaching from the Vital Essence of Liberation and the writings of the omniscient Drimay Özer [Longchenpa]. At the end of the meal you shape the leftovers into a *chong-bu* to offer [to the spirits]. Then you repeat the mantra that purifies the offering of the food [you received] and recite discourses [of the Buddha] to dedicate [the merit of the offering]. [Finally] you recite two prayers, *The Prayer for the Spontaneous Fulfillment of Wishes* and *The Prayer to Dispel Obstacles on the Path.*

[During the noon-time break,] you may read [aloud] profound discourses and tantras such as *Reciting the Names of Gentle Splendor* or *The Heart of the Perfection of Wisdom Discourse.* During times of mantra practice,[44] you should

---

[43] A *chong-bu* (*changs bu*) is a portion of food squeezed in the hand and then offered to the spirits.

[44] Here Kongtrul uses the term for intensive practice (nyen drup, *bsnyen sgrubs*) to indicate the practice of recitation of mantras during the visualization of deities.

continually recite mantras in a low voice without counting these in your total for the practice.

The Third Meditation Session

At the beginning of the afternoon meditation session, you quickly do the meditation, recitation of mantras, torma offering, and receiving the empowerment of the single form of Yangdak Heruka from the Secret Vital Essence cycle. Then you begin the main practice [of that period of the retreat].

The Afternoon Group Session

As soon as [the third] session is over, you must assemble at the sound of the drum in the protector temple called Cool Grove.[45] The protector ritual begins with the short version of *The Seven-Line Invocation of Guru Rinpochay* and the prayers that begin "Great bliss, profound and clear," "Pure from the origin," and "All the victors of the three times." Then you imagine the configuration of your own body as the Five Tantric Deities from the Shangpa Instruction Lineage. Mantras of the main deities are recited one hundred and eight times each and the others fifty times each. After the dissolution and reappearance [of the meditation deity], a torma is offered. Then the torma [offering] ritual of the Swift-Acting Fully Awakened Protector, *The Treasure Vault of Enlightened Activity*, is performed. The ritual for the creation phase meditation written in verse is added to the text. The meditations and recitations [of mantras connected to the practices] of the Inseparability of the Spiritual Master and the Protector, Eliminating the Darkness of [Broken] Commitments, and Taking Control of the Dakinis are all performed and a torma offered. The hundred-syllable mantra is recited twenty-one times during the practice of Eliminating the Darkness of [Broken]

---

[45] Kongtrul called the protector temple Cool Grove (Silway Tsal, *bsil ba'i tshal*), after the Indian charnel ground that is said to be the residence of Six-Armed Protector.

Commitments. All other mantras must be recited at least one hundred and eight times each.

Then the meditation of Vajra Black-Caped One with consort is done as written by the fourteenth lord [Karmapa, Tekchok Dorjay, in *The Brief Daily Practice of the Protector*]. [This includes] the recitation of one hundred and eight mantras and repetition of the mantras of torma offering to [the main deities], the five members of their entourage, and others. Following this, the Minling tradition ritual of *The General Torma Offering to the Committed Protectors* is performed. The fulfillment offerings to encourage the enlightened activity of the Protectress of Mantras and the Mamo of the Charnel Grounds should be added to the ritual.

Once these torma offerings are completed, you practice the following brief meditations and mantra recitations to prevent all general and specific interruptions to Buddhist practice: *The Heart of the Perfection of Wisdom Discourse* to prevent demons, the Lion-Faced [Dakini], the additional prevention, and Lokatri. All should be accompanied by clapping of the hands. A treasure text for the prevention of [interferences by] *damsi*,[46] *The Flaming Wheel*, should be recited and its mantra repeated seven times. Once *The Prayer to Prevent Untimely Death* has been recited,[47] the prayer for the long life of Jamgon Lama, Payma Garwang[48] written by Jamyang Kyentsay Wangpo (beginning "The guide of the three worlds") must be recited without missing a day. [The whole ritual is completed by] prayers common to all traditions for dedication of merit.

---

[46] *Damsi* (*dam sri*) are harmful spirits that are reincarnations of those who have broken their tantric commitments.

[47] Since the text mentioned here follows immediately after *The Flaming Wheel* in *The Treasury of Rediscovered Teachings*, I assume that it is the one Kongtrul is referring to. Another prayer in which the words "prevent untimely death" are repeated at the end of a number of supplications is included in *The Book of Common Prayer of the Oral Instruction Lineage of the Karmapas*, page 100b in the Palpung edition. The author's name is not mentioned.

[48] Jamgon Lama, Payma Garwang, is none other than Kongtrul himself.

The Fourth Meditation Session

The evening meditation session starts with a brief burnt offering [to the beings in the state between death and rebirth] and *The Prayer Given to Dorjay Dujom* [from *The Seven Prayers*]. [In conjunction with the prayer,] you imagine the visualized framework, the receiving of empowerment, the dissolution [of the visualization] and its melting into you. You then begin whatever meditation is the main practice of the retreat at that time.

After the Last Session

At dusk, when the session is over, the meditation and mantra recitation of Vajra Dagger of the Secret Vital Essence cycle is done. If you offer a torma, you also [meditate that you] receive empowerment. When you are particularly busy, it is possible to dispense with the three empowerments [of this meditation], however under no circumstances can the principal meditation and recitation of mantras be skipped.

Then, beginning with the visualized framework, you recite *The Prayer Given to the King* and *The Prayer Given to Mutri Tsaypo* [from *The Seven Prayers*]. You imagine receiving empowerment, dissolution [of the visualization] and its melting into you. You then perform an abridged form of [the meditation of] offering one's body [to the sources of refuge and to all beings].

Whenever convenient before or after [these meditations at the end of the day,] *The Twenty-five Vows* should be recited, changing the words [at the end of the lines] to words of acknowledgement of faults committed. *The Discourse of Three Clusters* and other prayers [of acknowledgement of fault] should also be recited at this time. As many prostrations as possible should be offered as you recite these prayers, except if the main meditation of the day has been withdrawal of the senses or mental stability within the Six Branches of Application, or the main practice of luminosity during Great Perfection meditation.

In general you should not acquiesce to [the force of habit of your] ordinary sense of self during sleep. It should be transformed into the spiritual path through techniques of the yoga of sleep, such as the transference of consciousness during sleep [to the realm of the Buddha] Boundless Light or [techniques you will learn] in conjunction with meditations on the Six Doctrines, Great Seal, and Great Perfection.

In the early morning you begin this daily schedule again with the yoga of waking from sleep, etc. Your exertion should be steady, avoiding either compulsive tension or lethargy.

From the time you begin the meditation of inner heat until the end of the retreat, you should regularly perform the physical exercises of Naropa and Niguma alternately. [These exercises are not done when your spare time is taken up by] memorial offerings and additional rituals or during periods [when the main meditation] is clear light, withdrawal of the senses, mental stability, or Direct Vision.

The physical exercises of the Six Branches of Application are too numerous and the period of this retreat too short to learn them well: you should simply accept that fact for now.

3. Extra Monthly and Yearly Rituals

BACKGROUND INFORMATION

The following two sections list the rituals that are performed each month or on a yearly basis. These lists and the descriptions of the rituals reveal Kongtrul's personal interests. Time was precious in his retreat: each of the choices of practices he made indicates his strong feeling that the practice or ritual was indispensable. As to the details of the rituals themselves, what we read here are concise scores of a number of tantric symphonies of the mind. The retreatants would practice meditation individually throughout most of the month; these rituals provided an opportunity for them to meditate together. As with a gathering of dedicated and proficient musicians playing a piece of music together, the whole is often much more than the sum of its parts.

Effective meditation in general and rituals in particular are felt to have both short and long-term beneficial effects on the environment. Tantric Buddhism believes that our thoughts, positive or negative, no matter how private or unexpressed, have an impact on the environment. The thoughts developed in the course of a tantric ritual are considered to have an extremely strong impact. The rituals originate in the inspiration of awakened or enlightened persons who have provided a framework for the uplifting of the mind to its full potential of awakening. The meditator enters the tantric world and is immersed in the awakened physical, verbal, and mental experience and presence of the deity. No participant in any of these rituals would ever conceive that it was being done for his or her benefit alone, nor would he or she imagine that its effect would be confined to the walls of the retreat center.

The main meditation of most rituals listed below are explicitly named, except for those on the tenth day of the month. These latter have Guru Rinpochay as their central figure. The practices — the Quintessential Vision of the Spiritual Master, the Quintessential Secret, and the Gathering of the Jewels — are all treasure teachings of meditation on different forms of Guru Rinpochay, the Indian master who succeeded in implanting and sustaining tantric Buddhist practice in Tibet.

Many of the special events of the year were memorial days of great masters of the past, held on the anniversary of their death according to the lunar calendar. Among these, Kongtrul's principal master, Payma Nyinjay Wangpo (the ninth Tai Situpa), was remembered every seventh of the month, although his death occurred on the seventh of the fifth lunar month. The thirteenth Karmapa, Düdul Dorjay, was one of the principal teachers of Payma Nyinjay Wangpo. One of the greatest of the Tai Situpas (the eighth), Chökyi Jungnay, is also remembered. His life was significant in that he founded Palpung Monastery and, for Kongtrul, that he was a master of many traditions of tantric meditation.

The founders of the Oral Instruction Lineage in Tibet — Marpa, Milarepa, and Gampopa — and the founder of the Shangpa Instruction Lineage, Kyungpo Naljor, were each remembered on their memorial days as was Orgyen Terdak Lingpa, the founder of Mindrol Ling Monastery of the Ancient Instruction Lineage, whose work Kongtrul admired and emulated. The remaining four figures honored by memorial days — Taranata, Rangjung Dorjay, Dolpo Sang-gyay and Longchenpa — join with Chökyi Jungnay as the most significant influences in Kongtrul's later writings. Of all of these masters, it is Taranata whose memorial day was given special attention: three days of rituals marked the event.

Of the special yearly events, the first and the last require some explanation. The memorial day of Milarepa is marked by the donning of cotton robes (ray bö, *ras 'bod*), a practice Kongtrul instigated during the second year of the first retreat (1862). During an entire winter night the retreatants wore only a cotton shawl and the very short uniform worn during the daily physical exercises, while meditating on inner heat and reciting the songs of realization of the masters of the Oral Instruction Lineage.

The last ritual of the year was a week-long offering to Six-Armed Protector. The requirements of this ritual are so demanding that, as was mentioned above in the section entitled "Entrance Into Retreat," eight persons were designated to come from Palpung Monastery for this occasion each year. Correct procedure for this ritual demands that a certain mantra be recited aloud continually — twenty-four hours a day — from the beginning to the end of the period of the practice, in this case one week. The retreatants would perform the actual rituals; the eight persons from the monastery shared the responsibility for maintaining the continuity of the mantras. The eight visitors would leave the retreat as soon as the rituals were completed.

In the Tibetan text for the following section, the program of the rituals and the meditations and prayers to be recited are described separately. Below the two sections have been integrated without omissions.

THE MONTHLY PROGRAM OF MEMORIAL OFFERINGS AND EXTRA RITUALS

On the Seventh Day of the Month

The seventh day of the [lunar] month marks the occasion of the memorial offering to our master, Buddha Vajra Holder [incarnate], Payma Nyinjay Wangpo. On this day, the Minling tradition offering practice of glorious Vajrasattva which unites canonical and treasure teachings is performed. On the seventh day of the fifth month in particular, the long prayer [describing his] life of freedom [is recited] and copious offerings must be made.

[The ritual of Vajrasattva] begins with *The Seven-Line Invocation of Guru Rinpochay* in the tradition of Chöwang, a prayer called *The Life of Freedom of Minling Terchen*, and the prayer [to Payma Nyinjay Wangpo] beginning "Upholding the instructions of Padmakara." [The main part of] the ceremony begins with the prayer to the lineage of Vajrasattva practice and includes the practice of visualization of oneself as the deity, the deity before one, and the deity in the vase; a fulfillment offering ritual; self-empowerment; a vajra feast offering; and *The Three-Part Torma Offering*. The offering of tormas to guardians of the doctrine is unnecessary during this ritual as these are offered each evening in the protector temple. To conclude [the ceremony], *The Prayer of Excellent Conduct* and *The Prayer of the Aspirations of the Bodhisattva Loving-Kindness* are recited.

On the Eighth Day

On the eighth day [of the month], the offering practice of the yogini Tara, [must be performed]. The ritual from Atisha's tradition [during which] the universe in a symbolic form is offered four times [and a similar ritual] from the New Treasures are done on alternate months.

The ritual [of Tara] begins with *The Homage and Offering to the Sixteen Elders* and the prayer to our master [Payma Nyinjay Wangpo] beginning "The incarnation of the compassion of all buddhas." After the entire offering ritual is completed, a prayer from *A Guide to the Bodhisattva's Way of Life* is recited.

On the Tenth Day

On every tenth day [of the month], a fulfillment offering through a vajra feast is performed [according to] *The Beautiful Garland of Flowers*, the activity ritual of the Quintessential Vision of the Spiritual Master. An offering of tormas to the guardians of the doctrine must be included with this ritual. On alternate months this ritual is followed by either the vajra feast offering of the practice of the spiritual master Vimalamitra or the reading of *The Heart of the Lotus Tantra* from the heart practice of the New Treasures.[49] [In particular,] on the tenth day of [the fourth lunar month] during which [the effects of acts] are multiplied by 100,000,[50] one hundred vajra feast offerings

---

[49] *The Heart of the Lotus Tantra* was discovered with the heart practice of the New Treasures, known as Dispelling All Obstacles (Barchay Kunsel, *bla ma'i thugs sgrub bar chad kun sel*), by Chok-gyur Daychen Lingpa.

[50] The fourth lunar month is particularly important for Himalayan Buddhists because they believe the Buddha's birth, death, and enlight-

are made during the ritual of the Gathering of the Jewels. On the tenth day of the fifth month, the vajra feast of the Quintessential Secret (discovered by the treasure revealer Chöwang) is performed along with *The General Fulfillment Offering to the Three Sources*.

The ritual [of the Quintessential Vision of the Spiritual Master] begins with *The Seven-Line Invocation of Guru Rinpochay* in the tradition of Daychen Lingpa, followed by the lineage prayer beginning "The buddhas of the three times." [The main ceremony] should be supplemented by the torma and fulfillment offering to guardians of the doctrine written by Karma Chakmay [*The Concise Daily Practice of Offering Tormas to Guardians of the Doctrine*]. Once [the reading] of *The Heart of the Lotus Tantra* and the meditation on the master Vimalamitra have been completed, a prayer for rebirth in the pure realm Blissful [Sukhavati; Day-wa-chen, *bde ba can*], beginning "All that is to be known," is recited.

On the Day of the Full Moon

On the fifteenth day [of the month], the offering ritual of the glorious Wheel of Time is performed. It begins with the following prayers: the abridged prayer to the omniscient one of Jonang and his spiritual heirs, and [prayers beginning] "In the presence of the buddhas," "The omniscient lord of spiritual life," "Great bliss, profound and clear," and "The incarnation of the compassion of all buddhas." After the inner offering has been consecrated,[51] [the main part of] the practice includes the offering ritual and the practice text of the nine deities [in the configuration of the Wheel of Time].

---

enment all occurred during this month. Thus the effects of actions are said to be multiplied by 100,000 during the month.

[51] The inner offering (nang chö, *nang mchod*) is alcohol representing what were considered by brahmin India to be the most defiled substances — five kinds of meat and five kinds of secretions from the human body. The consecration of the inner offering transforms these substances by the power of the buddhas into nectars charged with the potency of their wisdom.

Once the extensive ceremony is completed by offerings of tormas and a vajra feast, the prayer [for rebirth in the pure realm] Blissful written by Dolpo Sang-gyay [beginning] "Namo Lokeshvara" is recited.

On the Twenty-fifth Day

On the twenty-fifth day [of the month], the Shangpa Instruction Lineage offering practice to the five deities in the configuration of Wheel of Supreme Bliss is performed, together with the offering ritual of White or Red Celestial Woman, done alternately.

The ritual [of Wheel of Supreme Bliss] begins with prayers that [recount] the life of freedom of the noble one of Jonang [Taranata], both the autobiographical account [*The Wish-Fulfilling Tree of Faith*] and its supplement [*The Flower of Faith*]. Following the prayer to [Payma Nyinjay Wangpo] beginning "Upholding the instructions of Padmakara," the offering practice of Wheel of Supreme Bliss, self-empowerment, vajra feast, etc., are all done in their extensive forms. A vajra feast should be offered to White or Red Celestial Woman even if offerings are not distributed [among the retreatants]. At the end [of the day's rituals] *The Prayer of Great Seal Meditation* is recited.

On the Twenty-ninth Day

On the twenty-ninth day of the month, the first collective ritual is that of the Fully Awakened Six-Armed Protector. Supplementary texts are added to the main ritual [on this occasion]. The second collective ritual [of the day] is that of the Black-Caped One, *Vermillion*, to which fulfillment [offerings] are added. The third collective ritual is that of *The General Torma Offering to the Committed Protectors*. [This ritual] should also include [offerings to] the New Treasure protectors Swift-Acting Fully Awakened Protector, the Protectress of Mantras, the Queen of Existence, the Mamo of the Charnel Grounds, and Goddess of Longevity. Those protection and prevention [mantras and prayers] which are repeated daily without fail are also included in this ritual.

On the Thirtieth Day

On the day of the new moon [the following rituals are performed]: the offering practice of the nine deities [in the configuration of] great glorious Yangdak Heruka; *Ever-Excellent's Essential Activity* from the section on mind;[52] and the ritual which includes the reading of *The Secret Essence: The Tantra of Illusion*, during which a torma is offered. If there is not enough time to read this tantra during the six months of fall and winter when the days are shorter, *Chanting the Names of Gentle Splendor* must be read [in the course of the ritual which provides] the framework for the recitation.

[The ritual of Yangdak Heruka] begins with *The Seven-Line Invocation of Guru Rinpochay* in the tradition of Chöwang, the prayer called *The Past Lives of Minling Terchen*, a prayer which begins "The incarnation of the compassion of all buddhas," and a supplication to the lineage of Yangdak Heruka. Following these, mantra recitation and an offering of a vajra feast are done in full detail. After the tantra and *Ever-Excellent's Essential Activity* have been read, *The Prayer of Ever-Excellent* from the Northern Treasures is recited.[53]

Except for the offerings [to the protectors] on the twenty-ninth of the month, all the above ceremonies are done in two parts. The rituals on the tenth day of the month [and that of Tara] are done in the morning. All other rituals (offering practices) are performed during afternoon group sessions.

On both the full and new moon days of every month without exception, all the fully-ordained persons living in

[52] The section on mind (semday, *sems sde*) is the first of three divisions of teachings of atiyoga, the highest level of tantra in the Ancient Instruction Lineage.

[53] The Northern Treasures (Jang Ter, *byang gter*) includes treasure teachings discovered by Rikzin Godem Chen and Tulku Zangpo Drakpa.

the retreat center must gather with their outer monastic robe and mat to perform the purification and renewal of the vows of personal liberation,[54] including reading from the discourses [of the Buddha]. From the time the *ganti* stick[55] is beaten [as a summons] until completion of the ceremony with prayers of dedication of merit, [this purification and renewal] must not be performed casually, but must be carried out in an appropriate, dignified manner.

EXTRA OFFERING PRACTICES AND MEMORIAL OFFERINGS PERFORMED ON A YEARLY BASIS

The extensive version of the ceremony for the purification and renewal [of the three disciplines], *The Ladder to Freedom*, should be performed once daily from

- the second to the fifteenth day of [the first lunar month] (the miracle month)[56]
- the eighth to the fifteenth of [the fourth month] (of the constellation Arch)
- the first to the fourth of [the sixth month] (of the constellation First Invincible)
- the fifteenth to the twenty-second of [the ninth month] (of the constellation Horse-Head)

This ritual should be performed during the time usually allotted to the afternoon meditation session; however, if there is a special occasion, such as an offering practice, that

---

[54] The outer monastic robe (chögu, *chos gos*) and mat (ding, *gding*) are two of the requisite articles of fully ordained persons.

The vows of personal liberation include commitments accepted by laypersons and novice monks and nuns. This ceremony, however, is exclusively for the purification and renewal of the vows of full monastic ordination.

[55] The *ganti* stick is a long piece of wood beaten to summon monks and nuns to ceremonies relating to the vows of personal liberation.

[56] One time while living at Sravasti in northern India, the Buddha performed miracles during the first two weeks of the first lunar month, now called the miracle month (chotrul dawa, *cho 'phrul lza ba*) in the Tibetan calendar.

falls on the same day, the ceremony may be done at the beginning of the first collective session of the morning.

Special Practices Performed During the First Lunar Month

The fourteenth day of the miracle month is the occasion of an offering to noble Milarepa and the donning of cotton robes in his memory. [The temple] should be swept and offerings arranged on the shrine. [Your body] must be washed inside and out with the five nectars[57] and rubbed with a [fine] paste [of flour and butter]. All these preparations should be done according to correct procedure.

You should assemble in the main temple immediately after tormas have been offered in the protector temple that evening. As a preliminary, you recite a condensed version of *The Book of Common Prayer of the Oral Instruction Lineage of the Karmapas* including [a prayer called] *Loving Mind*; [prayers] in praise of Shakyamuni; development of the two forms of the mind of awakening; *The Homage and Offering to the Sixteen Elders*; [prayers in praise of] Marpa, Milarepa, Gampopa and the series of lives of the red and black crown spiritual masters [Shamarpa, Gyaltsab and Karmapa] and Tai Situpa.

Then you do the meditation on the master Milarepa, *Radiant Wisdom*, including the offering of a vajra feast. [During this ritual,] you recite the prayer calling him from afar and his mantra as many times as you wish. Once you have recited the preliminary practices [to the Six Doctrines] and done vase breathing, you maintain the meditation of inner heat. After donning cotton robes, you recite the entire ocean of songs of the Oral Instruction Lineage [of the Karmapas], *The Rain of Wisdom*. At dawn you perform the complete set of physical exercises [of Naropa].

[That day,] the fifteenth of the month, is the memorial day of Lord Marpa. During two group assemblies in the morning, the extensive ritual of purification and renewal of

---

[57] The five nectars (dutsi nga, *bdud rtsi lnga*) here refers to consecrated alcohol. Washing the inside of the body consisted of drinking a small amount of the liquid.

the three disciplines and the offering ceremony of *The Tantra of Adamantine Joy* are performed. During the afternoon the outer, inner, and secret meditations of the master Marpa are done together with self-empowerment and a vajra feast.[58]

On the twenty-fifth of the month, the memorial day of the noble Düdul Dorjay [the thirteenth Karmapa], prayers of praise and supplication to [this spiritual master] are offered during the [regularly scheduled monthly] offering practice.

Special Practices Performed During the Second Lunar Month

The second day of the month of the constellation of Later Reddish Stars is the memorial day of Orgyen Terdak Lingpa. At that time a fulfillment offering through vajra feasts in the tradition of the Heart-Essence of the Awareness Holders and the offering [ritual of] *The Secret Essence: The Tantra of Illusion* [are performed].

During the offering [ritual of Wheel of Supreme Bliss] on the twenty-fifth of the month, memorial offerings should be made to the omniscient Chökyi Jungnay [the eighth Tai Situpa]. Prayers of praise and supplication to this spiritual master [should be recited] and the ritual of reading *The Tantra of Wheel of Supreme Bliss* should be performed with a vajra feast after completion [of the day's meditation] on Wheel of Supreme Bliss.

The twenty-eighth of the month is the memorial day of the great noble one of Jonang [Taranata]. [To celebrate this,] the practice and offering ritual of the Five Tantric Deities from the Shangpa Instruction Lineage should be performed for three days, starting on the twenty-sixth.

---

[58] A self-empowerment (dak jook, *bdag 'jug*) is literally "to enter by oneself" into the configuration of deities. This is a common part of many offering rituals.

The Third Lunar Month

The entire full-moon day of the month of the constellation Brilliant should be spent performing the offering to *The Tantra of the Glorious Wheel of Time*, including the ritual during which the tantra is read and a vajra feast is offered.

The Fourth Lunar Month

During the first day of the month of the constellation Arch, *The Great Fragrant Smoke Offering of Gar* and [fragrant smoke offering rituals] from the New Treasures, or others as appropriate, should be performed in their full form as a food offering to the gods.

The Sixth Lunar Month

The fourteenth and the fifteenth days of the sixth month are the memorial days of the omniscient Rangjung Dorjay [the third Karmapa] and the incomparable [doctor] from Dakpo [Gampopa], respectively. However, a [monthly] offering [ceremony] is already scheduled for the fifteenth. [To celebrate these occasions,] the ocean of songs of the Oral Instruction Lineage [of the Karmapas, *The Rain of Wisdom*, should be recited] and a vajra feast offered on the fourteenth. Prayers of praise and supplication to Dakpo Rinpochay [should be recited] during the offering ceremony on the fifteenth.

The Ninth Lunar Month

The fourteenth of the ninth month is the memorial day of the learned and accomplished Kyungpo Naljor. [To celebrate,] a vajra feast should be offered in conjunction with *The Ritual of Offering to the Spiritual Masters of the Shangpa Instruction Lineage*. This should include the recitation of *Prayers Describing the Lives of Freedom of the Spiritual Masters of the Shangpa Instruction Lineage*.

The Tenth Lunar Month

The sixth day of the tenth month is the memorial day of the buddha of the three times, Dolpopa [Dolpo Sang-gyay]. On this day prayers of supplication to the father and spiritual heirs of the Jonang lineage [should be recited].

The Eleventh Lunar Month

At the end of the eleventh month, the permanent tormas that are arranged on the shrine in the protector temple must be replaced.[59] Additional offering rituals [for the protectors] must be performed in conjunction with this event. New tormas should be prepared on the twenty-fourth or twenty-fifth. On the evening of the twenty-sixth, the old tormas are [removed from the temple and] offered on the roof during the course of the usual ritual. Immediately thereafter, the new tormas are arranged and consecrated. For three or five days starting on the twenty-seventh, the extensive rituals of the main texts of the Swift-Acting Fully Awakened Protector (such as *The Treasure Vault of Enlightened Activity*) and [those of] [Vajra] Black-Caped One with his consort, entourage of five, and followers, must be scrupulously performed. *The Dancing Ocean of Accomplishment of the Ancient Instruction Lineage* must be recited, and fulfillment offerings to whichever [protectors of] the New Treasures must be [honored] are to be recited more than one hundred times each.

[59] Some tormas were offered and discarded daily; others, "the permanent tormas," remained for the whole year on the shrine. Although these were made from butter and roasted flour, the high altitude and low temperatures of the region prevented them from spoiling.

Special Practices Performed During the Twelfth Lunar Month

The eighteenth of the twelfth month marks the memorial offering to the omniscient Longchen Rabjam Zangpo [Longchenpa]. On this occasion the ritual of offering to the masters of the lineage of *The Heart-Essence [of Longchenpa]* should be performed in conjunction with a vajra feast.

The twenty-fourth of this month is dedicated to the preparations [for the year-end protector ritual]. On this day, tormas are made and arranged in the appropriate manner. Once this is done, the torma practice of the Swift-Acting Fully Awakened Protector, including the continual recitation of mantras, is performed for seven days (from the twenty-fifth until the morning of the second day [of the new year]). The necessary procedure and the order of [the prayers and meditations] to be recited during this time must be done as clearly described in the manual for this practice, without omissions, additions, or errors. The vajra of activity[60] must follow the [correct] procedures and [ensure that everything] is impeccably clean. The flour for the tormas, alcohol for the offerings, grains, blessed substances, and other necessary articles must either be given by the residence of the head lamas of the retreat or by the retreatants themselves. No other person's gifts may be added [to the offerings at this time].

The sound of the mantras recited should not be too loud (i.e., audible outside the retreat center), nor too soft (i.e., not audible near the persons reciting). [No one may] recite the mantras slower [than the rest of the group] during collective recitation. Those assigned to maintain the continuity of the mantras must not allow it to be broken by engaging in conversation or [indulging] in sleep. Arguments, dissension, and quarrels are completely unacceptable behavior [during this time]. The sounds [of the mantras] should not be audible from a distance, but should be easily audible close by. The pitch should be moderate, the speed even. The

---

[60] The vajra of activity (lay kyi dorjay, *las kyi rdo rje*) is the title of the shrine attendant.

recitation of the mantras sung aloud should be relaxed from the outset so as not to become gradually fatiguing.

At the end of the morning session at dawn on the second day [of the new year], the tormas are carried to the top of the [protector temple], led by incense and followed by a full procession. At that time no person, except those who came from the monastery, may be excused from reciting the prayers [with the others] in the courtyard. Once this concluding ritual is completed, all [the retreatants] must assemble in the temple to perform the extensive ritual for purification and renewal [of the three disciplines].[61]

---

[61] Kongtrul is making a very strong statement here. The lunar new year is the most important festival of the year for Tibetan-speaking people. Not only does it mark a new year, it is everyone's birthday. Tibetan people do not celebrate individual birthdays; everyone adds a year to his or her age after New Year's Day. The retreatants would have grown up with the expectation that this occasion would be an opportunity for a major celebration. Kongtrul is very clearly telling his retreatants to continue their meditation.

4. The Retreatant of the Protector Temple

BACKGROUND INFORMATION

The retreatant of the protector temple assumed responsibility for that temple and followed a program of meditation quite different from the other retreatants. He was usually someone who had previously completed a three-year retreat. Only two cycles of practices made up the three-year, three-fortnight program for this retreatant. Both are from treasure texts: the Gathering of the Jewels is a meditation on the outer, inner, secret, and very secret forms of Guru Rinpochay; the second, the Gathering of the Joyful Ones, is a meditation on the Eight Great Configurations of Deities, the main creation phase meditations of the Ancient Instruction Lineage.

In providing details of the second year of this retreatant's meditations, Kongtrul uses three technical terms — mahayoga, anuyoga, and atiyoga. Within the nine ways of spiritual development of the Ancient Instruction Lineage, these are the last three, the three stages of the inner tantras. Mahayoga meditations are mainly those on the creation phase; anuyoga, on completion phase; and atiyoga, on Great Perfection.

One of this retreatant's special duties was to leave the retreat on two occasions each year to perform special meditations and offerings.

During the fourth month, he would make offerings to the *nagas*, a class of beings which live in water and appear at its surface a number of times each month. Propitiation of the nagas is said to improve the weather and prevent certain diseases.

The place where the offerings were made was at the naga shrine. In 1859, before the area was opened as an area of sacred ground and before a temple was constructed, Kongtrul and Chok-gyur Daychen Lingpa made two shrines: one was dedicated to Mantra Protectress (one of the main protectors of the Ancient Instruction Lineage); the other was the naga shrine. Of the four streams in the area which, according to Kongtrul, made the sound of mantras as they flowed, this stream, the closest to the retreat center, made the sound of the mantra of Yangdak Heruka. Kongtrul describes the consecration of the shrine:

> When the great treasure revealer Chokling began the actual dedication of the shrines, the sky became clear and a marvelous rainbow appeared during a light rain like the descent of flower petals. An indication of the success of this shrine appeared: the flow of the eastern stream has since greatly increased. This shrine has been responsible for the pacification of all previous sicknesses and harm caused by the *nagas* in this area and in the whole region; new cases of the diseases have not appeared. Furthermore, the seasonal rainfall has been regular and crops and animals thrive. (*Catalogue*, page 18b)

The second occasion that the retreatant of the protector temple would leave the retreat was to commemorate Chok-gyur Daychen Lingpa's retrieval of treasure texts near the retreat in 1859. This event marked the inauguration of the area as sacred ground. In his autobiography, Kongtrul reports:

> On the tenth day of the sixth month, [Chok-gyur Daychen Lingpa] retrieved [some treasures] from the secret cave of Berotsana on the right side of Tsadra Rinchen Drak. These included the yellow parchment of the treasure texts of the three practices of the Secret Vital Essence and the guide to Tsadra, material for making the statue of great glorious [Yangdak Heruka], and consecrated substances to place inside it. (*Autobiography*, 96a)

The reader will notice that Kongtrul here records the month as the sixth; in this retreat guide and elsewhere, he writes that it was the fifth. Another inexplicable discrepancy in this story is the location of the texts: in other accounts, he writes that Chok-gyur Daychen

Lingpa retrieved the treasures in the secret cave of Guru Rinpochay.

In any case, the anniversary of the event was marked each year by the offering of many vajra feasts at six caves in the Tsadra area, each identified in the guide to the area as having been the meditation place of one of the great early masters of the Ancient Instruction Lineage.

The retreatant of the protector temple would be assisted at these times by the lama doing longevity practices. This person seems to have been a resident of the retreat center but not a participant in its programs. He was presumably performing longevity practices for Kongtrul himself.

THE PROGRAM FOR THE RETREATANT OF THE PROTECTOR TEMPLE

During the first two years [of the retreat, the retreatant of the protector temple] must complete all the practices of the phases of creation and completion which are contained in the profound instructions of Orgyen Laytro Lingpa's *Gathering of the Jewels*. To begin with, the blessing of union with the spiritual master's mind is meditated upon for three days. Then the four stages of the common preliminary practices are done for three days each, according to Sang-gyay Lingpa's [instructions]. Following this, one hundred thousand [repetitions of the prayer of] refuge, the prayer to develop the mind of awakening, the hundred-syllable mantra, the symbolic offering of the universe, and the short prayer to unite with the spiritual master's mind are all practiced according to the major commentary, *The Ornament of the Guru's Mind*. All these practices must be finished within a period of five months.

The following meditations [of the phase of creation] are practiced according to *Padmakara's Oral Instructions: A Guide to Mantra Practice. The Seven-Line Invocation of Guru Rinpochay* and the *vajra guru* mantra that are connected with it are each recited one hundred thousand times. The *tötreng tsal* [mantra][62] of the outer practice is then

[62] The tötreng tsal mantra (*thod phreng rtsal*) refers to a long mantra which includes one of the names of Guru Rinpochay, Payma Tötreng Tsal ("Lotus, Skull-Garlanded Adept").

recited three or four hundred thousand times. During the three months of the main practice, the inner stage, the mantra must be recited twelve hundred thousand times or more. The mantra of the secret practice, Wrathful Guru, must be recited four hundred thousand times; that of the very secret practice, Lion-Faced Dakini, three hundred thousand times. The meditations of the four forms of enlightened activity are done for three days each. The longevity practice is done for as long as time permits — either for three weeks or a month. During the completion of the practice by fire rituals, one tenth of the number of mantras [recited during] the Peaceful Guru practice must be recited. Once this is finished, practices of anuyoga and atiyoga that are related to the phase of creation are each meditated upon for a few days.

[The meditations of] the stage of completion are then done according to the manual, *The Complete Liberation of the Three Worlds*. The period of the year is divided among the various instructions [described in this text] so that each can be practiced until signs of success appear. Within that time, [the meditations] which are connected to the phase of creation of mahayoga and those related to the channels and energy winds of the anuyoga [system] are practiced for only a few days, as suitable.[63] On the other hand, all the special preliminary practices of atiyoga Great Perfection and its main practices — Cutting Through the Solidity of Clinging and Direct Vision — must be meditated upon for some months until some experience is achieved. At the end [of this period], transference of consciousness is practiced until signs of success appear.

Reading transmissions and instructions must be given [by the vajra master] for all the manuals of the meditations [mentioned above], as well as for supplementary texts and

[63] The channels (tsa, *rtsa*) are the passageways through which move the energy winds of the body. Tibetan and Chinese medical traditions describe precisely the actual network of the channels for the purpose of diagnosis and treatment; tantric meditations present various versions of the arrangements of channels that correspond to an ideal from the perspective of enlightenment.

the source texts [of the tradition]. At the beginning of the main practice [of the stage of creation], the empowerment-blessings of Peaceful Guru, Wrathful Guru, and Lion-Faced Dakini must be received together with the longevity empowerment and the command [to the protectors].

During the final year, as the appropriate empowerments, reading transmissions, and instructions are received, the intensive practice of the Gathering of the Joyful Ones, the great practice of the Eight Great Configurations of Deities, is performed. The activity ritual, *The Enjoyment of Great Bliss*, forms the basis [of the practice], while *The Great Manual of Mantra Practice* by the great translator Dharmashri describes its content. The explanation given in *The Sesame Oil Lamp*, a book that provides clarification [of Dharmashri's text], is followed for the practical details. The peaceful [mantras] are recited for only two weeks; the wrathful [mantras] for six months or more, up to a year, depending on the time available. [The practice] is completed by a burning-and-pouring [fire ritual] to produce a pacifying effect.

The lama of the protector area must remain in [the retreat compound] between retreats. [During that time,] an intensive practice of three months or more should be devoted to the full measure of mantras of the peaceful and wrathful aspects of Black Lord of Life from the New Treasures. Then if time permits, the full measure of mantras may also be recited for Vajra Dagger and Black Horse-Neck.

[During the retreat,] the retreatant of this temple must attend all group practices of annual and monthly offering rituals. The daily [supplementary] prayers and meditations described above that are done by all retreatants must also be recited without exception. There are some additions to that program:

After the recitation and meditation of White Tara during the morning session, the peaceful practice from the activity ritual of the Gathering of the Jewels must be recited along with the longevity practice, *The Iron Mountain*. At dawn brief burnt offerings to the gods, such as *The Mountain of Burnt Offerings* or *Billowing Clouds of Auspicious Virtue*, should be made.

At the end of the afternoon meditation session, the following practices are done: mantras for enlightened activity must be recited and fulfillment offerings made to Six-Armed Protector of the New Treasures; tormas are offered to the Three Yellow Deities and Great Glorious Goddess; and the mantra recitation, torma and fulfillment offerings to Goddess of Longevity are performed according to the activity ritual from the New Treasures. These practices are completed by the prayer that begins, "Guarding the doctrine of the Buddha."

At the end of the evening meditation session, the recitation for the Wrathful Guru, Lion-Faced Dakini, and the forms of enlightened activity must be done. In addition, fulfillment offerings through vajra feasts according to the practice of the Gathering of the Jewels must be offered without fail.

Recitation of mantras for enlightened activity and torma offerings must be performed on the fifteenth of [each lunar] month for Son of Renown [Vaishravana] of the New Treasures and on the twenty-eighth day for Consummate King of the Mamos.

For two days during the fourth month, at the time of the appearance of the nagas,[64] the lama of the protector temple and the lama doing longevity practices must alternately perform rituals at the site of the naga shrine. [The rituals include] *The Wish-Fulfilling Cobra*, the Sky Treasure offering to the eight great nagas, the offering to the nagas of the local springs written by Karma Chakmay, burnt offerings to the nagas, the fulfillment offering to the nagas,[65] and numerous repetitions of various torma offerings.

The tenth and eleventh days of the fifth [lunar] month are the anniversary of Terchen Rinpochay's [Chok-gyur Daychen Lingpa's] retrieval of profound treasures from the right side of this meditation place. The lama of the protector

---

[64] According to Tibetan astrology, the nagas appear on the 4th, 5th, 9th, 15th, 20th to 25th, and 30th days of the fourth lunar month.

[65] The text of the fulfillment offering is mentioned here specifically as a "*spang bskang*." I have not been able to discover the meaning of the word *spang* in this context.

temple (who is principally responsible) takes turns with the longevity-practice lama offering [a total of] one, two, or three hundred vajra feasts over a period of two days at six meditation caves [in the vicinity]: the three caves of the masters [Guru Rinpochay, Vimalamitra, and Humkara], and the three caves of Yeshay Tsogyal, Berotsana, and Namkay Nyingpo. [These vajra feasts are offered] according to the activity [rituals] of the two heart practices of the New Treasures,[66] the practice of the master Vimalamitra, the practice of the Eight Great Configurations of Deities called *The Lofty Palace* that was retrieved from Payma Shel Pook ["Crystal Lotus Cave"], the practice of Yangdak Heruka retrieved from Namka Dzö ["Treasury of Space"], and other practices.

Assistance required for the naga offerings, new articles for ordinary or special offerings, and other items needed at these times should all be ordered from the main lamas' residence [of the retreat] through the retreat attendant. It will also be necessary for the monastery to send a helper [for the lamas] during the two days of one hundred vajra feasts.

---

[66] The two heart practices (tookdrup, *thugs sgrub*) of the New Treasures are Dispelling All Obstacles (Barchay Kunsel, *bar chad kun sel*) and the Wish-Fulfilling Jewel (Yishin Norbu, *yid bzhin nor bu*). Both were discovered by Chok-gyur Daychen Lingpa and are classified by Kongtrul in *The Collection of Rediscovered Teachings* as meditations on the physically manifest body of enlightenment of the peaceful form of Guru Rinpochay.

5. General Rules of Conduct and Discipline

The vajra master is responsible for all facets of the spiritual life of the retreat center. He must bestow all the necessary empowerments, meditation instructions, and reading transmissions. In the beginning he must give instruction in the order of the prayers [recited collectively], the arrangement of the configurations [and offerings on the shrine], the melodies to be sung or played [during collective rituals], etc. Those unfamiliar with these skills must receive instruction so they become capable of performing them. During the retreat [the vajra master] must not ignore shortcomings in [correct procedure]. Without getting exasperated, he must carefully explain the reason [an improvement is necessary] and in this way immediately correct [any error]. In an extreme case, if it should happen that [a person] doesn't listen and causes a disturbance, the vajra master must prevent [the situation from continuing] by imposing appropriate disciplinary measures, such as [having the person] offer tea to the community or do one hundred prostrations.[67] The vajra master must care for all the retreatants as equals, without regard to previous familiarity or to partiality based on social class, influence, or wealth.

Everything given to this virtuous community — portions of tea and butter, general tea offerings, etc. — must be distributed to all without the slightest portion being wasted. The present or sure future value of all offerings, large or small, given by the faithful in general or with requests for special ceremonies in particular, must be fairly divided and distributed in equal shares among [the retreatants]. A portion of the yearly [budget] for the temple must be subtracted each month and given to the person responsible for the preparation of the offerings.

The [large] lamps that burn continuously and the others [offered] each evening in the temples should be checked [to see if they are still burning]. During the summer, the temple and retreat center roofs must be resealed; during the winter, the snow must be cleared away; and at all times dust must be swept from both the temples and the yard. When these things are obviously necessary, not doing them is wrong: you must arrange for them to be done immediately. Do whatever necessary to repair damage done to the temple by rodents. Don't ignore [what needs to be done]!

These points and the necessary practices described below have as their primary concern the preservation of both the structure and the contents of this center. The vajra master must assume the principal responsibility for this. The work that the vajra master must oversee — the yearly sealing of the roofs, repair of the ornaments on the temple roofs, the settling of [legal or other] disputes, etc. — should be referred to the spiritual heads, the treasurers, or the disciplinarians

---

[67] As is clear below, infractions of the rules were punished in a variety of ways: fines, prostrations, and even corporeal punishment. Of the three, the fines were undoubtedly the most effective deterrents. By the time any retreatant had reached adulthood, he had probably done enough prostrations as part of his spiritual practice that these were symbolic gestures of regret when given as punishment. As for corporeal punishment, this was probably meant more as a blow to the person's pride.

of the monastic administration who will give their immediate attention to these problems.[68]

All retreatants must be sure to own a cloak of patches, the outer upper and lower robes, and the monastic mat.[69] You may keep a begging bowl if you own one. You must also have the uniform for the physical exercises and a meditation belt. If possible, you may have a meditation hat made. From the time of the meditation of inner heat onward, no leather or fur may be worn under any circumstances; therefore, prepare clothes of heavy wool, etc. [before the retreat].

When prayers are being recited together it is best if the vajra master leads the recitation. If that is not possible, persons with good voices should take turns [leading the prayers]. The retreatants, the lama of the protector temple, and [the lama] performing longevity practices should each, in turn, assume the responsibility for ringing the gong to signal the beginning and end of meditation sessions. Within the protector temple, the arrangement of the offerings on the shrine, the making of tormas, the maintenance of the facility inside and out, etc., must be seen to by the lama of that temple alone.

A detailed accounting [of the contents of the retreat] must be carried out by one of the incarnate masters [of the main monastery] and the vajra master of this center during the period between three-year retreats. [During the retreat] the retreatants take turns assuming [the responsibility] for the preparation of the offerings. At the time of receiving the account book, the retreatant whose turn it is must make a careful comparison between what is recorded in the book

---

[68] The passage that follows has been given a different interpretation by every lama I have asked, so I am reluctant to include it in the translation. This seems the most likely: "They will resolve any questions according to the specific directives provided in the instructions written by the red and black crown spiritual masters together which carries their seal and which is accompanied by their orders to the guardian deities. One copy of their letter is here; another is in the office of the monastery."

[69] The cloak of patches (nam jar, *snam sbyar*) is an article of clothing worn only by fully ordained persons on special occasions.

and the actual contents of the temple. This should be done without the vajra master having to remind the retreatant to do so. Everything that is recorded in the account book, large or small, must be checked: the representations of the Buddha's body, speech, and mind; the offering utensils, the musical instruments, the tormas, and everything on the shrine; the boxes, cases, and other containers; even the ceremonial scarves. Whatever is found to be missing must be replaced with an identical item, regardless of whether or not the object in question is considered spiritually or materially valuable. If something is broken or damaged, it must be remade or repaired. If a cymbal or other musical instrument has been broken, it must be replaced.

[The retreatant responsible for the temple] must use the donations that were given expressly for offering practices, anniversary offerings, or daily offerings for their intended purpose. He should be sure to use everything as an offering without keeping even the smallest amount for himself. The shrine attendant must also sweep the inside and outside of the temple, wipe the offering bowls every day, and dust off or clean the other offerings from time to time. Water that has been offered should not be thrown out in unclean places — into [containers of] drinking water, on foot-paths, etc. It should be carried to where it can be disposed of in a clean place. The used tormas should be collected and given to the retreat attendant, who will barter them for juniper branches to be used during fragrant smoke offerings.

Each year there will be a collection from the retreatants as a group to buy two bricks of tea.[70] One should be used to buy whitewash to paint [the outside walls of] the retreat center. The other should be used to buy fragrant incenses, such as juniper branches, from behind the hill at Alo Paljor.[71] These should be finely ground and steeped in good alcohol. Once removed from the alcohol and dried, this incense can be used for daily or special offerings in both the

---

[70] Bricks of tea were useful and common currency at that time in the barter economy of eastern Tibet.

[71] Alo Paljor is a village between Palpung Monastery and the city of Dergay.

main temple and the protector temple. The vajra master must specify the time for making the incense and the retreat attendant must collect the necessary ingredients.

The daily tormas and offerings must be prepared by the person whose turn it is to do the work of shrine attendant. When there are special occasions when many offerings must be prepared, all those who are proficient at making tormas must lend a hand. For the special offerings during the fourth month and on other appropriate occasions, all the offering decorations, such as flags and banners, must be replaced. The old decorations are collected [and set aside] and new ones arranged in their place. As soon as the offering ceremony is over, the new decorations are collected and stored, and the old ones put back. For this sort of chore which requires immediate attention, all the retreatants are expected to help get the work done before noon-time.

Articles that are needed as offerings to the configurations of deities during offering practices should be removed [from storage] only at the time they are to be used. As soon as that period is over, they must be well taken care of by being returned to their containers, etc. It is not permitted to carelessly toss them to one side or to discard them.

Except for the times during rituals when it is actually necessary to rise for the offering of tormas or [portions of] the vajra feast, etc., the shrine attendant must not do anything that might break the continuity of the ritual, such as needlessly moving about or often getting up and then sitting down.

The leader of the prayers should not recite the prayers too slowly. This will make the session extend beyond the daylight hours or beyond the time everyone can sit comfortably. If the prayers are recited too rapidly for meditation to be done concurrently, the rituals will be of absolutely no use. Therefore, recite the prayers at a moderate speed. During the period of the year when the days are longer, the prayers may be sung to different tunes, and more time can be spent reciting mantras. During the months when the daylight hours are limited, prayers may be recited without a tune, and mantras recited for shorter periods of time. However, there is sure to be enough time during the daily collective morning ritual of purification and renewal [of the three disciplines] and during the evening ritual of torma offering for the prayers to be recited [properly] and some meditation to be done. You must never recite these rituals with such excessive haste that you are unaware of what words you've just recited. During the collective gatherings, the leader of the prayers should not have to carry the whole burden of recitation alone. All the residents of the retreat center are equally retreat lamas, and the recitation of these prayers is for your own benefit. Therefore, everyone should participate energetically while not forgetting the meditation to be done in conjunction with the prayers.

Most of the instruction manuals and the prayers to be recited have been printed: not acquiring them is senseless. You should collect all the necessary books before the retreat. There is no ritual whose order of prayers is too complicated to be learned: you should learn them well enough to be confident of the order of the rituals. No one has any reason to say "I haven't got that text," or, "I don't know the order of that ritual."

If there is someone among the retreatants with a good voice and a sound knowledge of the rituals, he may assume the responsibility for leading the prayers over a period of time. During that time he does not have to serve as shrine attendant. The ringing of the gong to signal the beginning and end of meditation sessions is done in turns. The beating of the drum [to signal] the beginning of the collective rituals, however, must be done by the shrine attendant. If there is no one who has a good voice and a sound knowledge of the rituals, the responsibility for leading the prayers must also be assumed in rotation.

When there are collective rituals, you must gather immediately at the sound of the drum. You remove your shoes on the porch before entering: no shoes may be worn in the temple. Rules of conduct in the temple are similar to those of [a temple in] any large monastery: one offers prostrations upon entering at any point before the end of the ritual, etc. During a ritual, you must not talk animatedly to one another, look around distractedly, sleep, rest by leaning one way or another, stretch your legs, cover your head, clean your nose, etc. You should remain in meditation posture and give your full attention to the prayers you are reciting and to the meditation. Except for the shrine attendant, no one may stand up during the ritual until a pause is announced.

At the beginning of a meditation session, the gong should be rung for some time, giving everyone enough time to hear it and to return to their rooms. At the completion of the session, the gong may be rung for a short time.

From the time when the list of retreatants is posted at the beginning [of the retreat] until it is taken down, no one, regardless of social standing, is permitted to enter the retreat. This includes ordained persons, laypersons, and, in particular, women. The single exception is the entrance of the eight persons who recite mantras continuously during the protector rituals at the end of the year. If [a retreatant has been responsible] for having an ordained person enter [the retreat] through the kitchen, the penalty is to make one hundred tea offerings [to the community].[72] If the person who entered was a layperson, the fine is to be paid in offerings of a ceremonial scarf and lamps. If it was a woman who entered, the chief spiritual guides of the monastery must be informed, and both physical and material punishment meted out. If a great disturbance has been caused by the entrance [of someone from outside the retreat], the retreatant responsible will be expelled from the retreat.

The group who enters to recite mantras continuously [during the year-end rituals] must consist of two leaders, lamas who have previously done the retreat, and six fully-ordained monks. They must arrive at the retreat during the day of the twenty-fourth [of the lunar month] and enter the protector temple after having been [purified] with consecrated scented water. They must leave on the second day

---

[72] There were two entrances into the retreat: one was above the retreat center, from Kongtrul's personal residence; the other was the door to the kitchen that the retreat attendant and the woodsman would use.

of the new year. They are not permitted to enter earlier nor to stay longer.

During the time [of the year-end rituals], it is not permitted for a retreatant to put his head out a window to the outside [of the retreat] or to look around at the sun, etc. [during the rituals]. If this has been done, the offender must offer between twenty-five and one hundred prostrations, depending on the severity of the offense.

Between retreats (i.e., once the list of retreatants has been taken down [at the end of the retreat]), the vajra master must give his prior permission for any visits to the temples by those whose visit is of significant importance. No one else is allowed to enter [the retreat enclosure]; visitors [not permitted to enter] may be met instead in the sitting room.

If a retreatant has a sickness that is not very serious, the attendant of the retreat may take care of him. Other retreatants should not interrupt their meditation practice on this account. If there is a case of serious illness, those concerned about and able to assist the retreatant must attend to and take care of him until his health improves.

The shrine in each person's room must be dusted, and the plates used for the symbolic offering of the universe, tormas, and any other objects, once cleaned, must be kept spotless. This symbolizes the purity of one's mind and contributes to the completion of the cultivation of merit and wisdom.

All your personal [belongings], such as religious paintings and statues, which have been recorded in the register should not be wasted through carelessness. You should present the list [of these objects] to the vajra master at the end of the retreat so that they can be returned to you without delay and in undamaged condition.[73]

No fire or flame except lit incense may be carried into any room. Even so, there are many tales of temples or possessions having been burnt by only the light of incense,

---

[73] According to Lama Gyaltsen (Kalu Rinpochay's nephew), the retreatants were not allowed to keep personal possessions for the duration of the retreat, even religious objects. These would be kept in storage and returned at the end of the retreat period.

so extreme caution and vigilance is necessary in carrying and placing it.

If any of the seats in the temples becomes tattered or punctured, the vajra master should be informed of it immediately. The materials needed for patches and sewing should be paid for from the general retreat account. New seats should be installed for each new retreat.

A very small amount of alcohol may be served at the time of the [protector] torma practice [at the end of each year] and during vajra feasts. Otherwise no alcohol in any form may be brought into this retreat center. Those who bring it in and drink will be punished: if the disturbance caused is major, a scarf and a brick of tea must be offered; for a minor offense, a tea [offering to the community] and one hundred prostrations must be offered.

In general, the retreatants should not be overly friendly with one another in the beginning. This can later become the cause of discord. Discord itself is meaningless: it breaks the commitments you have with your vajra brothers. Don't make playful jokes: jokes can lead to misfortune. Don't discuss your prejudices, be they positive or negative. [If you do] you'll become comfortable with these signs of your own limitations as a practicing Buddhist. Don't say things that express negativity in a concealed fashion: this spreads the meaningless disease of enmity. All [retreatants] should act in accord with the orders and wishes of the spiritual master.

You must wear the upper robe at all times, whether entering or leaving a room, or while sitting. Do not go to the collective assemblies without wearing the lower outer robe.

If a verbal fight has occurred, the person who started it must offer one hundred prostrations. The person who replied must offer fifty. If a physical fight has occurred, the first to strike will be caned fifteen times and must offer a brick of tea. The person who responded in kind will be caned ten times and must offer one quarter brick of tea. If many persons were involved in a serious fight or if a retreatant has struck the vajra master, this must be reported to the head spiritual guides of the monastery. If the offense has been serious, the offender will be expelled from the retreat as well as being given an appropriate punishment. Those who ignore the vajra master's directives and contradict him must offer tea and one hundred prostrations.

When the attendant has signalled that tea is served, you may leave your room to take tea and to go to the washroom. When the start of a meditation session is signalled, you must return to your seat and start your practice of virtue. No one is to leave his room from the time the meditation session has been signalled until the end of the session. The penalty for leaving the room [during this time] is twenty-five prostrations. [The penalty for] talking to one another once the meditation session has begun is ten prostrations for each person involved in the conversation. After the session has begun no one — including the two retreat attendants — may visit any of the retreatants until the end of the session. The attendant must keep watch. The penalty for leaving the room is ten prostrations. If the circumstances are exceptional, the person who must visit another should first explain the special importance of the business he has to the vajra master. If the vajra master considers the request and agrees that the circumstances are exceptional, the retreatant may visit [the other's room].

Once the meditation session has begun and [meditations] involving recitation, such as the preliminary practices, are being done, the sound of each retreatant's recitation must be clearly audible. In the case of [meditations without recitation], such as the clear light stage of the Six Doctrines, you must concentrate single-mindedly on the subject of the meditation. No one is permitted to plant thorns in the peace of mind [of their neighbors] by acting differently from the group — remaining silent when prayers or mantras should be recited, or audibly reciting them during periods of silent meditation, etc.

No alterations in the recitations and meditations as presented in this manual can be made according to the wishes of anyone, including the vajra master and the leader of the rituals. The Fully Awakened Protector of Cool Grove, Blazing Fire, has already been empowered [to act] if this occurs.[74] The retreatants must never create their own foolish styles [of program] by picking and choosing [their favorite practices]. However, [if a retreatant] has [recitations and meditations] that must be performed daily because of previous commitments of empowerments, reading instructions, or meditation retreats, these may be done in their shortest form between meditation sessions, whenever convenient. No alteration of the main practices is permissible.

At dawn and at night everyone must play the hand drum, bell, thigh-bone trumpet, etc., according to the signal [marking the beginning or end] of the meditation session. Doing as one likes — playing the instruments much earlier

---

[74] The Fully Awakened Protector of Cool Grove, Blazing Fire (Yay-shay Gonpo Sil-tsal May-bar, *ye shes mgon po bsil tshal me 'bar*) is the name of a statue of Six-Armed Protector, which Kongtrul calls "the main statue of the protectors" in the temple. He explains:

> As it is stated in the secret treasures,
>
> *Samaya!*
> This statue of the glorious protector
> Was fashioned by Nagarjuna from clay of the naga's realm
> And consecrated as the black *heruka.*
> When Nagarjuna was practicing at Cool Grove,
> Its blazing fire vanquished the non-Buddhists.
> In order that it might guard the Buddha's doctrine in the future,
> I conceal this as a precious treasure.
> *Samaya!*
>
> This particularly sacred likeness of the *heruka*, the secret [form of] the protector, wonderful and radiant with blessing, was given to me by Orgyen Chok-gyur Daychen Lingpa as foretold in the text. This [master], an embodiment of enlightenment who is the chief of an ocean of revealed treasures, retrieved the statue when he opened the great secret treasury at Yelpuk Namka Dzö.
>
> [The treasure text] promises that wherever it resides, the statue provides refuge from the eight or sixteen dangers, particularly those of fire and water. Furthermore, it bestows ordinary or supreme accomplishments according to one's prayers, exactly as one wishes, and can liberate beings through being seen, heard, remembered, or touched. The statue of the protector called Blazing Fire is similar to a wish-fulfilling jewel. (*Catalogue*, page 63b)

Kongtrul placed it at the heart of a larger statue of Six-Armed Protector in the protector temple.

or later than everyone else, or sometimes playing them and sometimes not — is not permissible.

No form of distraction — reading books, writing letters, sewing, etc. — may be indulged in, under any circumstances, during the last part of a meditation session. Even those who are repeating the three-year retreat and who are familiar with the program must receive specific permission from the vajra master before using time from the meditation sessions to perform any important work that serves the temple or the community as a whole. Apart from this, [even persons repeating the retreat] may not use this time, under any circumstances, for activities such as painting, sewing, or carpentry. Short, practical letters such as are necessary may be written only during the periods between meditation sessions. If someone has been told clearly by the vajra master not to do some form of work during the last part of the meditation sessions and does not follow his instructions, the tools used must be confiscated.

Those persons who are unfamiliar with Buddhism may study, on entering the retreat, those texts of the program mentioned above as being indispensable and specifically those textbooks explaining the three disciplines. Apart from those few books, no study, research, or examination of any texts concerning the major or minor subjects of the study of Buddhism is permitted under any circumstances. Study, reflection, and mental training are ordinarily considered vital [to our spiritual lives]. However, when the practice of meditation is our major concern, the many sources of discursive thought [intrinsic to study] act as obstacles to our [development of] meditative experience. Because one session of valid meditation practice is far more valuable than an entire lifetime devoted to study and reflection, we here are satisfied with wholehearted meditation practice.

All members of the retreat, beginning with the vajra master and including the lama of the protector temple and the retreatant doing longevity practices, must attend without exception all the [group assemblies of] offering practices, [monthly or yearly] offering ceremonies, and the regular daily rituals. Except in the event of sickness and two [consecutive] absences for specific important work for which the vajra master has given permission, not even one absence from the group assemblies can be excused.

The rules of conduct for the lama of the protector temple and the retreatant doing longevity practices are identical to those for the rest of the retreatants, with the exception of the special recitations [they must perform]. The lama of the protector temple must beat the drum continuously when reciting the prayers at the beginning and end of the meditation sessions and during the fragrant smoke offering ceremony each morning.

The vajra master is responsible for supervising all the community possessions, particularly the tea and butter that is distributed. Without wasting even as much as a needle, the retreat attendant must distribute to the temples and to each of the retreatants the full extent of whatever offerings were received. This must be done fairly and without favoritism.

Red paint for the [outside of] the temple must be given by the head lamas' residence. The payment in bricks of tea for whitewash and the similar payment for the above-mentioned incense must be deducted from the community accounts.

The retreat attendant is responsible for storing community property, including that which is to be distributed and the offerings from the faithful. [The attendant] must also prepare tea, cook soup, and draw water [for the retreatants' use]. Each morning he must sweep and collect the dust from inside [the buildings] and from the yard. [He must] reseal the roofs of the temples and all other buildings [during the summer]. He must take care of the repair of the buildings, such as checking the drains along the eaves of the roofs. The attendant's work should be dedicated to giving appropriate attention to the major and minor needs [of the retreatants]. During the periods between meditation sessions he should visit and report to the retreatants concerned. All of these duties should be carried out conscientiously and consistently.

If [the attendant] has shown extreme partiality in giving

a great portion of the community property to a relative or friend, or if [the attendant by words or actions] makes an important patron of the retreat unhappy, wrathful ceremonies should be performed in the protector temple [to correct the situation]. If [the attendant] has obviously wasted community property, is serving poor tea [i.e., withholding food in order to deceive], and using community property for himself, the reason for it must be explained to and assessed by the assembly of the retreatants. Material equal to the value of the wasted goods must be returned [to the community].

When tea is taken by the retreatants, it must be served hot.[75] The meal served at noon must be made during the latter part of the morning meditation session with whatever ingredients are available. [The attendant] must be skillful and energetic in always ensuring that no food is wasted. Because there is only one attendant, the retreatants should not make many requests of him (such as for special food) when he is very busy, such as when there are extra ceremonies taking place, or during the winter when he has to clear the snow [from the courtyard].

[In the kitchen,] the pots and pans that are not in immediate use should be well stored. Those in immediate use should be kept carefully washed. [The cook] should keep his hands and the dishtowels clean.

If a box or leather container in the storeroom or in other places [in the retreat] has been seriously damaged, the storekeeper himself must provide a replacement. Of course, the same is true for all the bronze or copper pots and pans and other utensils used in the kitchen.

The woodsman only serves this retreat center and is not in the employ of the main lamas' residence so there should never be any change in the amount of firewood available. In addition [to his main work,] the woodsman should serve the vajra master and the retreatants and help the attendant in his spare time. This might include resealing the roofs of the buildings and whitewashing the walls during the

---

[75] There is a short unclear passage at the beginning of this sentence concerning the boiling of the butter and tea which is served.

summertime, clearing away the snow in winter, or going to the monastery for whatever errands might be necessary. He should be rewarded by being given tea, food, more than one person's share [of the offerings distributed to the community], and tokens of appreciation from the vajra master.

During the seven days of protector practice at the end of the year, the woodsman must continually help the attendant and remain awake during the night meditation session. At that time it will be impossible for him to collect firewood so it must be stored in advance.

The two retreat helpers must not be deceitful, undependable, or abusive to those of lesser position [outside the retreat]. For as long as they stay at this retreat center, they must serve everyone impartially and consistently. They must speak to both the vajra master and the retreatants clearly and honestly. Any form of disrespect such as aggravation, angry words, or foul language is never permitted. The penalty for any inappropriate speech — contentious or foul language, etc. — to the vajra master is a tea offering to the community and one hundred prostrations.

If "the bad become mighty and oppress the good," [i.e., if either retreat helper] never provides any suitable service and begins to be physically abusive, the main lamas' residence must be informed and asked for assistance. According to the gravity of the offense and disturbance caused, appropriate physical and material punishment must be meted out. If the disturbance caused is major, the attendant must be expelled and after he has been replaced, wrathful punishment must be called for from the protectors.

If persons appear in the vicinity of the retreat (i.e., within the border of the paths that define this area) to cut grass or trees, or to hunt birds or deer, they must be prevented from doing so. The sovereign Karmapa and his spiritual heirs, the great treasure revealer Chok-gyur Lingpa, and many other outstanding individuals have often given their command [protecting this area, so such trespassing] is totally forbidden. You must do what you can to prevent their activity and guard this area. However, if the person is obstinate and destructive you must immediately invoke wrathful force in the protector temple by waving the black flag on which their names have been written, etc.

The retreatants, for your part, should not thoughtlessly regard the two retreat helpers as your servants nor should you be rudely forceful [in your requests]. You should calmly request work in your service while being considerate of their spare time and ability.

The main point is that all [in the retreat community] — master and students — must not become inconsiderate, selfish, or given over to thinking mainly of this life's needs. Your main focus should be whatever genuine form of spiritual practice you are engaged in. This place, with its representations of the Buddha's body, speech, and mind, is a pillar of the doctrine of the Oral Instruction Lineage. You should think that you must not waste [your time here] as you sit on your meditation cushion. With such a thought you will prevent yourself from both dashing your hopes for this and future lives and from becoming the object of others' scorn or ridicule. Three years is a very short time: you should concentrate on making some progress [on the spiritual path] and on successfully finishing the retreat.

THE MOST CRUCIAL ADVICE FOR LIFE IN RETREAT

The master, your spiritual guide, performs the acts of the Buddha directly before you. Treating him with even subtle disrespect physically, verbally, or mentally will cause sickness and many other misfortunes during this lifetime. [This disrespect] will be the beginning of all undesirable experiences, such as [finding that whatever] skill or talent you have developed is of no use to yourself or to anyone else. [In addition], once this life is over you will experience many lifetimes of lengthy, intense, and intolerable suffering [within the cycle of] existence.

Therefore, those who have entered this retreat should behave as is advised in the excellent teachings of the Buddha: Having decided not to act disrespectfully toward the spiritual master, active expression of your admiration through service to him should increase. Having decided not to speak ignobly, such as describing your spiritual guide's faults in order to make vapid jokes, you should always remark admiringly on his qualities. In this and other ways, verbal expression of your esteem should increase. Mentally, you should repeatedly reflect on the qualities and kindness of the spiritual master. In this way, the boundless inspiration and respect you feel will increase.

Expressed succinctly, [you should follow] the tradition of the noble Naropa, the noble Milarepa, and the other precious teachers of our Oral Instruction Lineage. You should never think negatively of the spiritual master and never disregard his instructions. You should make the inspiration and respect you feel the sole basis of your practice of meditation.

When the spiritual master teaches, everyone must have left their shoes [outside the temple]. In this retreat center it is a rule that each teaching must be preceded by the full offering of the universe in symbolic form. [Such an offering] is essential. Whether the teaching is long or brief, you must give your full attention to it and listen appreciatively. During all empowerments and blessing ceremonies in particular, your repetitions of the prayers should be precise and your concentration on each detail of the visualizations impeccable.

You should ensure that you are able to remember all the instructions in the visualizations [of the meditation practices]. If you have not been able to grasp the meditation during the lesson because you are below average, you should request special instruction to clarify the specific features of the visualization that you do not understand. [It is possible to meditate without] intellectual understanding of the essential points, but if you are doubtful about [the details of] the meditation itself, [your efforts] will be fruitless. Therefore it is essential that you consult [the master] immediately to alleviate your doubts.

If time permits, the spiritual master should examine the retreatants' comprehension of the meditations from the time of the preliminary practices until the end of the retreat period. Although that might be impossible, he should consider the retreatants his students and act accordingly. This includes continually receiving and noting the retreatants' reports of their experiences and signs in the practice of the Six Doctrines, the signs that appear [during the Six Branches of Application practices of] withdrawal of the senses and mental stability, the way [the experience of] the meditations of Great Seal and Cutting Through the Solidity of Clinging develop, and the emergence of Direct Vision. If they have not developed [these experiences, the master must give guidance] in how to correct errors in meditation so that they arise. [If a retreatant] lies, claiming falsely that he has had a certain experience, the spiritual master must correct this by stating that such deceit is unacceptable. [The master must also impart instructions] concerning the removal of obstacles to and the enrichment of meditative experience appropriate to each retreatant's spiritual development. The spiritual master must give encouragement to maintain their practice to those who are able to meditate well and who have developed some experience. The spiritual master should always give whatever instruction is necessary to augment the positive and to pacify the negative [elements in the retreat]. He should untiringly do whatever is helpful [for the retreatants], such as not ignoring from the outset any sickness that a retreatant might have and arranging for it to be treated by whatever means are at the disposal [of the retreat community].

Our teacher, the victorious compassionate Buddha, gave an unlimited amount of advice concerning the life of fully ordained persons staying in retreat. A brief example is found in *The Mound of Jewels Discourse*:

> Kasyapa, when a solitary fully ordained person has gone into retreat and lives a solitary life, he or she should develop love toward all beings through eight forms of activity. What are these eight? They are benevolent love, cheerful love, good-humored love, sincere love, non-discriminating love, harmonious love, love that appreciates the uniqueness of each thing, and love that is as pure as the sky. Kasyapa,

> love toward beings should be developed through these eight forms of spiritual activity.
>
> Kasyapa, a solitary fully ordained person should develop this attitude: "I have come here from such a great distance. I am alone, without any companion, so whatever I do, good or bad, will neither be praised nor criticized by anyone. However, the gods, nagas, spirits, and honorable buddhas are aware if I am single-minded or not. Because they are my witnesses while I live here in retreat, may my mind not become unvirtuous! May I understand that all my present preoccupations with desire, my preoccupations with anger, and my preoccupations with other forms of unvirtuous acts are just ordinary discursive thoughts. May I not become indistinguishable from those who delight in much entertainment! May I not become indistinguishable from those who live in the cities and suburbs! If I do become indistinguishable from them, I will have deceived the gods, nagas, and spirits, and become displeasing to the buddhas. However, if I live according to spiritual values in retreat, the gods, nagas, and spirits will not criticize me and I will become pleasing to the buddhas." This is the attitude to be developed.

It is also advised that [while in retreat] you should live purely, maintaining perfect ethical conduct while giving steadfast enthusiastic effort to the teachings of the four truths, the twelve links of causation, and the [thirty-seven] aspects of awakening.[76] The omniscient Rangjung Dorjay has written:

---

[76] These subjects, mentioned only by name in this quotation, are explained in detail elsewhere, particularly in *The Jewel Ornament of Liberation*: The four truths are of suffering, the origin of suffering, its cessation, and the path toward that cessation (see *Jewel Ornament*, note 16, page 237). The twelve links of causation are a description of the coming-into-being of cyclic existence (see pages 192-95). The thirty-seven aspects of awakening are "topics essential for realizing enlightenment" (see note 15, pages 138-39). The four levels of mental stability and formlessness are the meditative absorptions of the highest gods (see pages 80-81). The world of desire comprises all the realms of sentient beings except for that of the highest

How wonderful, in this dark and troubled time,
You fortunate ones who wish to practice in retreat!

These days, since everyone has a short life with many shifts of fortune
And little time for great undertakings,
You may not have had a complete education.
But as long as your devoted faith is constant,
And you always develop intense compassion toward others,
Stay in retreat and maintain strong enthusiastic effort.

As stated in the supreme tantras of the direct path,
Always single-mindedly practice faultless and one-pointed meditation
On the phase of creation and on all the pith instructions
Concerning the channels, the energy winds, and the mind of awakening.[77]

Once you have meditated on the absorptions of the four levels
Of mental stability and formlessness, and gained realization,
Do not rest in that state, but enter the world of desire
And, as in an illusion, perform the six perfections until their completion.

May the arising of ignorance and other causal links unravel naturally, without contrivance.
Having realized the Great Seal, that the self is without essence,
And rejecting the contentment of perfect peace,

---

gods (see note 9, page 10-11). The six perfections are generosity, ethical conduct, patience, enthusiastic effort, mental stability, and appreciative discernment (see chapters 11-17). The ten stages of awakening are levels of spiritual development traversed before full enlightenment (see chapter 19). The five paths lead a person from the entrance into Buddhist practice to enlightenment (see chapter 18).

[77] Here "the mind of awakening" is a term equivalent to "vital essence." See note 34 above.

May you work for the benefit of others until the cycle of existence is emptied.

If you practice meditation in this way,
The ten stages of awakening, the five paths, the aspects of awakening,
Superior vision, higher awareness, infinite meditative absorptions,
The strengths, the forms of courage, and the eighteen unique qualities[78]
Will all be perfected through reliance on your spiritual guide.

You should take this advice to heart as if it were nectar.

The shortcomings of not staying in retreat are mentioned in *The Discourse to Inspire Noble Aspirations* where twenty disadvantages of enjoying distractions [are described]. *The Discourse to End Lapses in Ethical Conduct* and other [discourses] state that the negative effect of distractions can lead to the experience of suffering in the three miserable existences for innumerable lifetimes.[79]

The benefits of staying in a meditation retreat are mentioned in *The Lion's Roar of Venerable Loving-Kindness Discourse*:

> Kasyapa, a bodhisattva might completely fill the expanse of a great thousand, three-fold thousand world system with flowers, incense, scented powder, and perfume to offer them to the Buddha three times a day and three times a night for one hundred thousand years. Compared to having made that offering, far more merit is produced by a bodhisattva having taken seven steps in the direction of a hermitage because he or she is apprehensive and fearful of distracting worldly talk, fearful of [the state

[78] The eighteen unique qualities (ma dray pa chöjay, *ma 'dres pa bco brgyad*) are qualities of the Buddha alone: six qualities of his physical presence, six of his understanding, three of his enlightened activity, and three of his wisdom.

[79] The three miserable existences are those of the hells, the starving spirits, and the animals.

> of life within] the entire three worlds, and intent on working for the benefit of others.
>
> Kasyapa, what do you think about this? Is the Buddha joking? Or trying to deceive [you]? If you think that this can't be the speech of the Buddha, you should not think so, Kasyapa. Why is that? Because [the truth of this] is clearly apparent to me.

The outstanding qualities [of meditation in retreat] compared to scholarship are mentioned in *The Reunion of Father and Child Discourse*:

> A person might study this definitive teaching of the bodhisattva's meditative absorption during ten aeons and explain it to others, but it is far more meritorious to have meditated upon it for the space of time it takes to snap the fingers.

The Supreme Meditative Absorption Discourse states:

> The Honored One spoke to Ananda, "Even if you don't attain any of the four results of virtuous practice[80] through meditation on absorption in mental stability, it is a million times more noble [to have done this meditation] than to become learned."

That [meditation in retreat] is superior to other offerings is stated in the same text:

> One leaves the home life and practices the path of
> spiritual development
> Serving[81] the victorious, supreme human being
> With food, drink, religious robes,
> Flowers, incense, and balms.
>
> Another, anguished by [the transitory nature of]
> composite phenomena,
> Turns toward a hermitage and takes seven steps

---

[80] The four results of virtuous practice (gejong gyi draybu shi, *dge sbyong gyi 'bres bu bzhi*) are stream-enterer, once-returner, non-returner, and *arhant*.

[81] The text reads "has not served" (*rim gro byas ma yin*); I have assumed *byas pa yin* to be correct.

With a sincere wish to awaken for the benefit of others.
This one gains merit far superior to the first.

Moreover, the results of the three ways of spiritual development [within Buddhism] are quickly attained by staying in retreat. However, if none of these are achieved during this lifetime due to deficient merit and effort, it has been said repeatedly that [its effect] will bring an end to dissipation and neutralize the obscuring emotions before the time of three buddhas has passed. Because similar statements have been repeated countless times by [masters of the past], you should earnestly give your innermost concern exclusively to the practice of meditation in retreat.

III. Words of Advice for Life After Retreat

You should satisfy yourself by [ensuring] that the result of your spiritual practice is not wasted. How can this be done?

These days, we can't really expect to achieve accomplishment or even the beginnings of [the signs of] heat.[82] We're just ordinary individuals who must practice [toward the realization of] enlightenment in a simple manner.

Once you've stayed the full time in the retreat center, you receive the title of spiritual master (lama). If you imagine this to be sufficient for you to carelessly accept offerings from the faithful or on behalf of the deceased, and you feel content with the meditation practice you have done, this is more repugnant than [if you were to support yourself with] the profit from the sale of animals you slaughter.

You have now found the path to liberation. You should recognize and acknowledge that this is thanks to the

---

[82] The signs of heat (drö, *drod*) refer to abilities that develop when a meditator progresses beyond the initial stages of spiritual development. This term does not refer to physical warmth.

kindness of the spiritual master and [to your own] virtuous good fortune. In order to not waste these good karmic propensities [you possess], you should not apathetically abandon the creation and completion meditations you have done here for as long as you live.

The best [thing for you to do] is to sever all worldly bonds of attachment and to do a retreat alone to take [your practice] to its fruition. Second-best is to promise yourself to never support yourself in ways that are contradictory to spiritual life, and then to practice meditation for the full extent of your life, serving the spiritual master and Buddhism and doing whatever is beneficial for others or meaningful to your own spiritual life. The least [you can do] is to never barter your three years of retreat for food or clothing, thus irreparably harming yourself in this life and the next. Instead, you should be certain to always keep in mind some practices that purify [negative acts] and augment and refine [your merit and awareness].

In general, wherever you go or reside after your stay in this retreat center — to a monastery or out into the world — you should physically never be without the clothing of ethical conduct; verbally, recitation of prayers and mantras; and mentally, love, compassion, devotion, respect, pure view, and the meditative absorptions of the phases of creation and completion.

You should always maintain a sincere wish to help others. You should conscientiously apply yourself to meditation during the first and last parts of the day, instead of sleeping. You should never indulge in wrong forms of livelihood such as flattery, hinting, manipulation, hypocrisy, and giving with expectation of receiving something in return. You should be content with just as many clothes as will cover your body, just as much food as will sustain you, and whatever shelter and sleeping place you find. You should continually reduce your preoccupations. Whatever happiness or misfortune you experience should be integrated into your spiritual life through [whatever technique] is suitable to your ability — be it mind training, equanimity, or [meditation on] emptiness, etc.

Making false claims of having seen gods or demons, having higher perception, having accomplished signs of success in meditation, etc., is to misrepresent one's experience as being special when in fact it is ordinary. Not only do such lies break your vows, they also contradict the final commands of the former great masters of the Oral Instruction Lineage. Never tell [such] lies.

Never drink alcohol, whether you are at home or elsewhere.

You should avoid like poison selfishness, attachment or aversion to the eight worldly concerns, self-contented pride, lack of consideration for others, etc.[83] Assume as humble a position as possible. Focus your attention on your spiritual master and the sources of refuge. Train yourself to have a pure view [toward all persons] impartially. Adopt the lifestyle of the former great masters of the Oral Instruction Lineage. Be conscientious and confident in firmly upholding this retreat center's tradition of spiritual practice.

In summation, *The Discourse to Inspire Noble Aspirations* states:

> Loving-Kindness, if an individual of the Bodhisattvas' Way has four qualities, he or she will not be harmed or troubled at the time of the destruction of the sacred instructions of the Buddha during the last five-hundred-year period of this era but will become joyfully liberated. What are these four qualities? They are recognition of one's own faults; refusal to discuss the faults of other individuals who are of the Bodhisattvas' Way; not [to give special] attention to the homes of friends, family, or those who give one alms; and not to say unpleasant words. Loving-Kindness, if an individual of the Bodhisattvas' Way has these four qualities, he or she will not be harmed or troubled at the time of the destruction of the sacred instructions of the Buddha during the last five-hundred-year period of this era, but will become

[83] The eight worldly concerns are toward gain and loss, happiness and misery, praise and blame, fame and obscurity.

joyfully liberated.

Moreover, Loving-Kindness, if an individual who is of the Bodhisattvas' Way has four qualities, he or she will not be harmed or troubled at the time of the destruction of the sacred instructions of the Buddha during the last five-hundred-year period of this era, but will become joyfully liberated. What are these four qualities? They are to completely renounce the attitude of the Lesser Way; to avoid accruing an entourage; to stay on the outskirts of settlements; and to energetically seek self-discipline, quietude, and mental tranquility. Loving-Kindness, if an individual of the Bodhisattvas' Way has these four qualities, he or she will not be harmed or troubled at the time of the destruction of the sacred instructions of the Buddha during the last five hundred year period of this era, but will become joyfully liberated.

Therefore, Loving-Kindness, if an individual of the Bodhisattvas' Way wishes to eliminate all the obscurations of past acts and wishes not to be harmed or troubled at the time of the destruction of the sacred instructions of the Buddha during the last five-hundred-year period of this era, but to become joyfully liberated, he or she must not delight in distraction; must stay in isolated places, in forests, or on the outskirts [of settlements]; must completely overcome the laziness due to neglecting [the welfare of] others; must recognize his or her own shortcomings without examining the faults of others; must enjoy remaining silent; and must delight in resting in the perfection of appreciative discernment.

However, should such an individual develop the wish to indicate [this practice] to others, he or she should maintain a non-materialistic frame of mind and should bestow the gift of spiritual instruction [without thought of reward].

This is the Buddha's advice. Even at such a late date as this, if you believe it and put it into practice, you can quickly attain the mastery of the state of a great monarch of spiritual life who spontaneously contributes to the welfare of one and all. This is the true speech [of the Buddha] and is completely reliable.

Dedication and Colophon

The force of disengagement lights the fire of enthusiastic effort,
Eradicating the darkness of confusion with the dawn of wisdom.
May an endless series of buddhas, lions among men,
Appear in this ever-existing, everlasting world during my lifetime.

The Buddha's excellent speech, an infinite array of wish-fulfilling jewels,
Is rejected by the uncivilized people of this darkened time.
What good to them is this trinket of counsel for conduct?
Yet some may appear who will value these words.

For those destined ones may this book afford sight of freedom,
And for others may it be a precious lamp
Illuminating the way of good conduct.
May it long light the path to liberation!

This book was written in order to clarify the behavior appropriate to those dedicated to the profound practice [of meditation] in [the place] called The Ever-Excellent Abode of Radiant Great Bliss, the isolated retreat of Palpung Monastery, the great headquarters of the Oral Instruction Lineage in Do-Kham (Eastern Tibet). It was written by an impersonator of a holder of the lineage of meditation practice in degenerate times, [named] Karma Ngawang Yonten Gyatso Trinlay Kunkyab Palzangpo [Jamgon Kongtrul].[84] May this work contribute to the spread, growth, and endurance of the precious instructions of the lineages of meditation practice.

May virtue and well-being increase!

---

84 Karma Ngawang Yonten Gyatso Trinlay Kunkyab Palzangpo (*karma ngag dbang yon tan rgya mtsho phrin las kun khyab dpal bzang po*; "Eloquent Ocean of Qualities Whose Glorious, Excellent Enlightened Activity is All-Pervasive"), the name Kongtrul uses when signing this text, was given him when he accepted monastic ordination at Palpung Monastery.

Appendix 1
Books Referred to in the Introductory Sections

The list below is of the texts the translator referred to in the introduction or in the additional information included with the details of the program of the retreat.

The Autobiography of Jamgon Kongtrul (*phyogs med ris med kyi bstan pa la 'dun shing dge sbyong gi gzugs brnyan 'chang ba blo gros mtha' yas kyi sde'i byung ba brjod pa nor bu sna tshogs mdog can*) by Jamgon Kongtrul. *Collected Works*, Volume 16, pages 59-478.

The Catalogue of the Structure, Sacred Contents, and Spiritual Life of the Isolated Retreat of Palpung Monastery (*dpal spungs yang khrod kun bzang bde chen 'od gsal gling rten dang brten par bcas pa'i dkar chag zhing khams kun tu khyab pa'i sgra snyan*) by Jamgon Kongtrul. This book gives a complete picture of the history, life, and contents of his retreat center. *Collected Works*, Volume 11, pages 3-256.

A Concise Classification of Empowerments, Blessings and Related Ceremonies (*dbang bskur byin rlabs sogs kyi rab dbye nyung bsdus blo dman nyams dga'*) by Jamgon Kongtrul. *Collected Works*, Volume 9, pages 179-196.

A Concise Manual for the Practice of Severance (*lus mchod sbyin gyi zin bris* [sic] *mdor bsdus kun dga'i skyed tshal*) by Jamgon Kongtrul. *The Treasury of Precious Instructions of Tibetan Buddhism*, Volume 16, pages 387-405.

The Empowerment of Entering as a Child (*dpal dus kyi 'khor lo sku gsung thugs yongs rdzogs kyi dkyil 'khor du byis pa 'jug pa'i dbang bskur bklag chog tu bkod pa ye shes rgya mtsho'i bcud 'dren*) by Jamgon Kongtrul. This long text is not included within any of *The Five Treasuries*.

The Encyclopedia of Buddhism has two parts, a root text and a commentary. All the quotes in this text have been taken from the commentary called *The Infinite Ocean of Knowledge* (*shes bya kun la khyab pa'i gzhung lugs nyung ngu'i tshig gis rnam par 'grel ba legs bshad yongs 'du shes bya mtha' yas pa'i rgya mtsho*) by Jamgon Kongtrul. Beijing: People's Press, 1985.

The Guide to the Sacred Ground of Tsadra Rinchen Drak (*thugs kyi gnas mchog chen po de vi ko tri tsa 'dra rin chen brag gi rtogs pa brjod pa yid kyi rgya mtsho'i rol mo*) by Jamgon Kongtrul. *Collected Works*, Volume 11, pages 477-546.

The History of the Source of the Profound Treasures and the Treasure Revealers (*zab mo'i gter dang gter ston grub thob ji ltar byon pa'i lo rgyus mdor bsdus bkod pa rin chen bedurya'i phreng ba*) by Jamgon Kongtrul. *The Treasury of Rediscovered Teachings*, Volume 1, pages 291-760.

An Impartial History of the Sources of Spiritual Instruction (*ris med chos kyi 'byung gnas mdo tsam smos pa blo gsal mgrin pa'i mdzes rgyan*) by Jamgon Kongtrul. This book includes a short history of the Bön religion. *Collected Works*, Volume 9, pages 69-100.

Jamgon Kongtrul's Retreat Manual (*dpal spungs yang khrod kun bzang bde chen 'od gsal gling gi sgrub pa rnams kyi kun spyod bca' khrims blang dor rab gsal phan bde'i 'byung gnas*) by Jamgon Kongtrul. *Collected Works*, Volume 11, pages 257-320.

The Last Days of the Life of Jamgon Kongtrul (*rje kun gzigs 'jam mgon ngag gi dbang phyug yon tan rgya mtsho'i zhabs kyi 'das rjes kyi rnam par thar pa ngo mtshar nor bu'i snang ba*) by Tashi Chöpel continues the story of Kongtrul's life until his death and funeral. *Collected Works of Jamgon Kongtrul*, Volume 16, pages 479-524.

Meaningful to Behold (*zab lam rdo rje'i rnal 'byor gyi khrid yig mthong ba don ldan*) is a text of instructions in the Six Branches of Application by Taranata. *The Treasury of Precious Instructions of Tibetan Buddhism*, Volume 17, pages 133-231.

Nectar Appearing in a Mirage: A Partial Account of the Story of Payma Garwang (*'dus shes gsum ldan spong ba pa'i gzugs bsnyan padma gar gyi dbang phyug phrin las 'gro 'dul rtsal gyi rtogs pa brjod pa'i dum bu smig rgyu'i bdud rtsi*) by Jamgon Kongtrul. *Collected Works*, Volume 15, pages 261-342. The title of the book is an example of Kongtrul poking fun at himself.

The Ornament of the Guru's Mind (*rdzogs pa chen po yang zab bla sgrub dkon mchog spyi 'dus kyi khrid yig gu ru'i dgongs rgyan nyin byed snying po*), by Tsaywang Norbu, is a text of instructions in the practice of the Gathering of the Jewels. *The Treasury of Rediscovered Teachings*, Volume 8, pages 177-280.

The Prayers to be Recited During the Preliminary and Actual Practices of the Shangpa Instruction Lineage (*ye shes mkha' 'gro ni gu las brgyud pa'i zab lam gser chos lnga'i sngon rjes ngag 'don rdo rje'i tsig rkang byin rlabs 'od 'bar*) by Jamgon Kongtrul. *The Treasury of Precious Instructions of Tibetan Buddhism*, Volume 11, pages 29-45.

The Proclamation of the Prophecies (*lung bstan mdo byang*), presumably a treasure discovered by Chog-gyur Daychen Lingpa.

The Prophecy of the Dakinis of the Three Sources (*rtsa gsum mkha' 'gro'i lung bstan*), presumably a treasure discovered by Chok-gyur Daychen Lingpa.

The Ritual of Offering to the Spiritual Masters of the Eight Great Practice Lineages (*sgrub brgyud shing rta chen po brgyad kun 'dus kyi bla ma mchod pa'i cho ga byin rlabs dngos grub yon tan kun gyi 'byung gnas*) by Jamgon Kongtrul. *The Treasury of Precious Instructions of Tibetan Buddhism*, Volume 16, pages 1-65.

The Secret Transmission of the Dakinis (*mkha' 'gro'i gsang lung*), presumably a treasure discovered by Chok-gyur Daychen Lingpa.

A Supplement to the History of the Lineages (*khrid brgya'i brgyud pa'i lo rgyus kha skong*) by Taranata. *The Treasury of Precious Instructions of Tibetan Buddhism*, Volume 18, pages 99-116.

The Torch of Certainty (*phyag chen sngon 'gro bzhi sbyor dang dngos gzhi'i khrid rim mdor bsdus nges don sgron me*) by Jamgon Kongtrul. *The Treasury of Precious Instructions of Tibetan Buddhism*, Volume 8, pages 3-124. Translated into English by Judith Hanson (Boulder: Shambhala, 1977).

Appendix 2
Books and Prayers Mentioned in the Retreat Manual

Kongtrul mentioned many texts in his manual, but only those named by either title or author have been listed. The letter K or T and a number following some books' names indicate their order within *The Collection of the Buddha's Word* (K for the Tibetan name for this collection, *Kangyur*) or *The Collection of Treatises* (T for the Tibetan name, *Tengyur*) as they are listed in the *Catalogue of the Tibetan Buddhist Canons (bKa' 'gyur and bsTan 'gyur)*, edited by Prof. Hakuju Ui et al. (Sendai, Japan: Tohoku Imperial University, 1934).

"All that is to be known" (*she bya ma*), also called *The Aspiration to Travel to the Blissful Pure Land* (*bde ba can du bgrod pa'i smon lam*), was written by Dayshin Shegpa, the fifth Karmapa. Included in *The Book of Common Prayer of the Oral Instruction Lineage of the Karmapas*, pages 108b-110a in the Palpung edition.

"All the victors of the three times" (*dus gsum rgyal kun*) is a supplication written by Minling Terchen to himself.

The Beautiful Garland of Flowers (*bla ma dgongs pa 'dus pa las phrin las lam khyer bsdus pa me tog phreng mdzes*) is the activity ritual for the Quintessential Vision of the Spiritual Master, discovered by Sang-gyay Lingpa. *The Treasury of Rediscovered Teachings*, Volume 7, pages 387-416.

Billowing Clouds of Auspicious Virtue (*rgyun gyi bsangs mchod dge legs sprin phung*) is an offering to the beings in the state between death and rebirth, by Jamgon Kongtrul. *Collected Works*, Volume 12, pages 487-504.

The Book of Common Prayer of the Oral Instruction Lineage of the Karmapas (*dpal ldan karma bka' brgyud kyi rjes su 'brang ba'i dge 'dun rnams kyi thun mong tshogs su zhal 'don du bya ba'i chos spyod kyi rim pa legs lam rab gsal*) compiled by Chökyi Jungnay, the eighth Tai Situpa. Published in Palpung and Rumtek monasteries.

The Brief Daily Practice of the Protector (*mgon po'i rgyun khyer bsdus pa*) is a text for offering tormas to the protectors of the Oral Instruction Lineage of the Karmapas by the fourteenth Karmapa, Tekchok Dorjay.

"The buddhas of the three times" (*dus gsum sangs rgyas*) is a supplication to the lineage of the practice of the Quintessential Vision of the Spiritual Master. Author not mentioned. *The Treasury of Rediscovered Teachings*, Volume 9, pages 379-80.

The Complete Liberation of the Three Worlds (*rdzogs pa chen po yang zab bla sgrub dkon mchog sphyi 'dus las: rdzogs rim khrid yig khams gsum yongs grol*) contains the instructions for the stage of completion meditations associated with the Gathering of the Jewels. By Jamgon Kongtrul. *The Treasury of Rediscovered Teachings*, Volume 8, pages 281-362.

The Concise Daily Practice of Offering Tormas to Guardians of the Doctrine (*bla ma dgongs 'dus kyi bka' srung chos srung gter srung gi gtor tshogs rgyun khyer bsdus pa*) for the practice of the Quintessential Vision of the Spiritual Master. By Karma Chakmay. *The Treasury of Rediscovered Teachings*, Volume 7, pages 421-40.

The Dancing Ocean of Accomplishment (*bstan pa skyong ba'i dam can chen po rnams kyi phrin las dngos grub kyi rol mtsho*) is an offering ritual for the protectors of the Minling tradition. By Gyurmay Dorjay and Dharmashri. *The Treasury of Rediscovered Teachings*, Volume 39, pages 43-148.

The Discourse of Three Clusters (*'phags pa phung po gsum pa zhes bya ba theg pa chen po'i mdo*) (K284). Translated as *The Sutra of Three Heaps* by Brian C. Beresford in *Mahayana Purification* (Dharamsala: Library of Tibetan Works and Archives, 1980).

The Discourse to End Lapses in Ethical Conduct (*sangs rgyas kyi sde snod tshul khrims 'chal pa tshar gcod pa'i mdo*) (K220).

The Discourse to Inspire Noble Aspirations (*lhag pa'i bsam pa bskul ba'i mdo*) (K69).

The Enjoyment of Great Bliss (*sgrub chen bka' brgyad bde gshegs 'dus pa'i las byang bde ba chen po'i rnam rol*) is the activity ritual for the Gathering of the Joyful Ones of the Eight Great Configurations of Deities. By Gyurmay Dorjay. *The Treasury of Rediscovered Teachings*, Volume 14, pages 185-238.

Ever-Excellent's Essential Activity (*kun bzang don phrin*). I have been unable to find this text; this translation of the name reflects guesswork on my part.

Fifty Verses in Praise of the Spiritual Master (*bla ma lnga bcu pa*) by Aryasura (T3721). Translated into English and published as part of *The Mahamudra Eliminating the Darkness of Ignorance* by Alexander Berzin (Dharamsala: Library of Tibetan Works and Archives, 1978).

The Flaming Wheel (*phir zlog 'khor lo 'bar ba'i gzhung man ngag dang cas pa'i skor rnams*) The text for prevention of *damsi* was discovered by Tulku Zangpo Drakpa; it is included in a longer text of instructions by Jamyang Kyentsay Wangpo. *The Treasury of Rediscovered Teachings*, Volume 45, pages 197-228.

The Flower of Faith (*rje btsun rin po che'i rnam thar gsol 'debs kha skong dad pa'i me tog*) is a supplement to Taranata's life story in verse, by Jamgon Kongtrul. *The Treasury of Precious Instructions of Tibetan Buddhism*, Volume 12, pages 453-56.

The Fourteen Root Downfalls (*rdo rje theg pa'i rtsa ba'i ltung ba bcu bzhi pa'i 'grel pa*) by Lakshmikara (T2485).

The General Fulfillment Offering to the Three Sources (*rtsa gsum rab 'byams kyi bskang rin chen 'bar ba'i phreng ba*) is mainly a text of offerings to the protectors; by Tsaywang Norbu and Pawo Dorjay Tsuglak Gawa. *The Treasury of Rediscovered Teachings*, Volume 41, pages 157-70.

The General Torma Offering to the Committed Protectors (*dam can spyi'i gtor ma'i chog nyung ngur bsdus pa*) by Gyurmay Dorjay. *The Treasury of Rediscovered Teachings,* Volume 41, pages 1-14.

"Great bliss, profound and clear" (*bde chen zab gsal*) is a collection of supplications by Taranata to himself.

The Great Fragrant Smoke Offering of Gar (*sgar bsangs chen mo yid bzhin dbang rgyal dngos grub char 'bebs*) by Palden Drakpa Chokyang, compiled from the writings of the second, third, and ninth Karmapas. Published at Palpung Monastery.

The Great Manual of Mantra Practice (*sgrub chen bka' brgyad bde gshegs 'dus pa'i bsnyen pa'i go don lag len dang cas pa'i yi ge rin chen sgron me*) instructions for the practice of the Gathering of the Joyful Ones of the Eight Great Configurations of Deities. By Dharmashri. *The Treasury of Rediscovered Teachings,* Volume 14, pages 1-88.

The Great Path of Awakening (*theg pa chen po'i blo sbyong don bdun ma'i khrid yig blo dman 'jug bder bkod pa byang chub gzhung lam*) is a commentary on *The Seven Points of Mind Training.* By Jamgon Kongtrul. *Collected Works,* Volume 8, page 614-60. Translated into English by Ken McLeod (Boston: Shambhala, 1987).

Great Seal: The Ocean of Certainty (*lhan cig skyes sbyor gyi zab khrid nges don rgya mtsho'i snying po phrin las 'od 'phro*) is a meditation teacher's manual by Wangchuk Dorjay, the ninth Karmapa. Published at Palpung and Rumtek monasteries.

"Guarding the doctrine of the Buddha" (*sangs rgyas bstan srung*) is a prayer recited daily by the lama of the protector temple. Text not located.

"The guide of the three worlds" (*'jig rten gsum mgon ma*) is a prayer for the long life of Jamgon Kongtrul written by Jamyang Kyentsay Wangpo. Text not located.

A Guide to the Bodhisattva's Way of Life (*byang chub sems dpa'i spyod pa la 'jug pa*) (T3871) by Shantideva. Translated into English by Stephen Batchelor (Dharamsala: Library of Tibetan Works and Archives, 1979).

The Heart of the Lotus Tantra (*padma'i snying po'i rgyud*) is found in *The Treasury of Rediscovered Teachings,* Volume 42, pages 297-300, included within *The Ritual for the Recitation of The Heart of the Lotus Tantra.*

The Heart of the Perfection of Wisdom Discourse (*bcom ldan 'das ma shes rab pha rol tu phyin pa'i snying po*) (K21). Numerous translations into English have been made of this discourse.

Homage and Offering to the Sixteen Elders (*gnas brtan phyag mchod*) by Pandit Shakya Shri. Included in *The Book of Common Prayer of the Oral Instruction Lineage of the Karmapas*, pages 32a-33b (Palpung edition).

"In the presence of the buddhas" (*rgyal ba mdun ma*) is also called *The Supplication to the Omniscient Father and Spiritual Heirs of the Jonang Lineage* (*kun mkhyen jo nang pa chen po chos rje yab sras rnams kyi gsol 'debs byin rlabs can*) by Nya-Ön Kunga.

"The incarnation of the compassion of all buddhas" (*rgyal ba yongs kyi*) was a prayer for the long life of Payma Nyinjay Wangpo, the ninth Tai Situpa, written by Pawo Tsuklak Gawa and made into a supplication by Tekchok Dorjay, the fourteenth Karmapa, after the death of Payma Nyinjay. Published at Palpung Monastery.

The Iron Mountain (*padma 'od 'bar tse sgrub lcags kyi ri bo gud du phyes nas bskur tshul bltas chog bsdus te byas pa*), a longevity practice by Karma Chakmay. *The Treasury of Rediscovered Teachings*, Volume 8, pages 81-92. This is the empowerment connected with this practice; I have been unable to find the practice text itself.

The Jewel Ornament of Liberation (*dam chos yid bzhin nor bu thar pa rin po che'i rgyan*) by Gampopa. Translated into English by H.V. Guenther (Boston: Shambhala, 1959).

The Ladder to Freedom (*tsogs gsog gi rim pa dang rjes su 'brel pa'i sdom pa gsum gyi gso sbyong rgyas bsdus thar pa'i them skas*) is a ritual for purifying and renewing the three disciplines by Jamgon Kongtrul. *Collected Works*, Volume 13, pages 177-226.

The Life of Freedom of Minling Terchen (*gter chen chos kyi rgyal po'i rnam thar gsol 'debs zhal gsungs ma*) by Gyurmay Dorjay (Minling Terchen himself). *The Treasury of Rediscovered Teachings*, Volume 3, pages 261-66.

The Lion's Roar of Venerable Loving-Kindness Discourse (*'phags pa byams pa'i seng ge'i sgra chen po bstan pa'i mdo*) (K67).

The Lofty Palace (*dam chos rdzogs pa chen po sde gsum las: gsang skor yi dam bskyed rim dang byang bu khrigs su bsdebs pa*) is a treasure teaching of the practice of the Eight Great Configurations of Deities discovered by Chok-gyur Daychen Lingpa. This text was written by Jamyang Kyentsay Wangpo. *The Treasury of Rediscovered Teachings*, Volume 58, pages 571-86.

Loving Mind (*sems btse ma*) is a prayer taken from a passage in *The Ornament of the Discourses* (*theg pa chen po mdo sde'i rgyan*) by the bodhisattva Loving-Kindness (T4020).

"The master who holds the vajra" (*bla ma rdo rje 'dzin ma*) is a prayer to acknowledge faults in one's behavior. Included in *The Book of Common Prayer of the Oral Instruction Lineage of the Karmapas*, pages 12b-13a in the Palpung edition. Author not mentioned.

Meaningful to Behold (*zab lam rdo rje'i rnal 'byor gyi khrid yig mthong ba don ldan*) is a text of instructions in the Six Branches of Application by Taranata. *The Treasury of Precious Instructions of Tibetan Buddhism*, Volume 17, pages 133-231.

The Mound of Jewels Discourse (*'phags pa rin po che'i phung po zhes bya ba theg pa chen po'i mdo*) (K88).

The Mountain of Burnt Offerings (*rig 'dzin srog sgrub las ri bo bsang mchod*) is a text for offerings to repay karmic debts, first heard in the sound of the hand-drum Lhatsun Namka Jikmay played when he was opening an area of sacred ground in Sikkim. *The Treasury of Rediscovered Teachings*, Volume 43, pages 569-72.

"Namo Lokeshvara," also known as *The Prayer for Rebirth in the Blissful Pure Land* (*bde ba can du skye ba 'dzin pa'i smon lam*), was written by Dolpo Sang-gyay.

Offering a Vajra Feast to One's Own Body (*padma'i zhal gdams grol thig mthong ba rang grol las: rang lus a nu'i tshogs mchod*) is a combination of a treasure teaching and a text by Longchenpa on meditation to accompany meals. *The Treasury of Rediscovered Teachings*, Volume 41, pages 127-30.

"The omniscient lord of spiritual life" (*kun mkhyen chos rje*) is a supplication by Dolpo Sang-gyay to himself and thirteen of his disciples who, he said, were his equals.

The Ornament of the Guru's Mind (*rdzogs pa chen po yang zab bla sgrub dkon mchog spyi 'dus kyi khrid yig gu ru'i dgongs rgyan nyin byed snying po*) is a text of instructions in the practice of the Gathering of the Jewels by Tsaywang Norbu. *The Treasury of Rediscovered Teachings*, Volume 8, pages 177-280.

Padmakara's Oral Instructions: A Guide to Mantra Practice (*yang zab dkon mchog spyi 'dus kyi bsnyen yig bklag chog tu bkod pa padma'i zhal lung*) is a text of instructions in the practice of the Gathering of the Jewels, by Jamgon Kongtrul. This book should have been part of his *Collected Works* but is missing from Kyentsay Rinpochay's edition. Published by Palpung Monastery.

The Past Lives of Minling Terchen (*chos rgyal gter bdag gling pa'i 'khrung rab kyi gsol 'debs ngo mtshar rgyan gyi me tog*) by Jamgon Kongtrul. Published by Palpung Monastery.

The Prayer for the Spontaneous Fulfillment of Wishes (*bsam pa lhun grub*), a prayer by Guru Rinpochay given to Prince Mutri Tsenpo, is a treasure text discovered by Tulku Zangpo Drakpa and transcribed by Rikzin Godem Chen. Although discovered separately from *The Seven Prayers*, it is considered to be the seventh of that series and has been printed with it in *The Treasury of Rediscovered Teachings*, Volume 5, pages 172-86.

The Prayer of Ever-Excellent (*kun tu bzang po'i smon lam stobs po che*) was discovered by Rikzin Godem Chen. *The Treasury of Rediscovered Teachings*, Volume 60, pages 733-39.

The Prayer of Excellent Conduct (*bzang po spyod pa'i smon lam*), from *The Flower Ornament Discourse*. Translated by Thomas Cleary in *The Flower Ornament Scripture* (Boston: Shambhala, 1987), Volume 3, pages 387-94.

The Prayer of Great Seal Meditation (*phyag chen smon lam*) by the third Karmapa, Rangjung Dorjay. Included in *The Book of Common Prayer of the Oral Instruction Lineage of the Karmapas*, pages 110a-111b in the Palpung edition.

The Prayer of the Aspirations of Loving-Kindness (*byams pa'i smon lam*) is a passage contained in the forty-first chapter of *The Pinnacle of Jewels Discourse* (*dkon mchog brtsegs pa chen po chos kyi rnam grangs*) (K45).

The Prayer to Dispel Obstacles on the Path (*gsol 'debs bar chad lam sel*) is a treasure text discovered by Chok-gyur Daychen Lingpa; *The Treasury of Rediscovered Teachings*, Volume 10, pages 51-58.

The Prayer to Prevent Untimely Death (*srung 'khor gnam lcags rdo rje'i thog chen log 'dren klad 'gems zhes bya ba zab mo dag snang gi skor*) was written by Lhatsun Namka Jigmay. *The Treasury of Rediscovered Teachings*, Volume 45, pages 229-38.

Prayers Describing the Lives of Freedom of the Spiritual Masters of the Shangpa Instruction Lineage (*dpal ldan shangs pa bka' brgyud kyi ngo mtshar rin chen brgyud pa'i rnam thar gsol 'debs u dumba ra'i phreng ba*) by Jamgon Kongtrul. *The Treasury of Precious Instructions of Tibetan Buddhism*, Volume 12, pages 389-448.

"Pure from the origin" (*gdod nas rnam dag*) is a supplication written by Payma Nyinjay Wangpo to himself.

Radiant Wisdom (*rje btsun ras pa chen po la brten pa'i bla ma'i rnal 'byor tshogs mchod dang bcas pa ye shes dpal 'bar*) is a meditation on Milarepa by Jamgon Kongtrul. *Collected Works*, Volume 1, pages 457-72.

A Rain of Blessings (*bla ma'i rnal 'byor byin rlabs char 'babs kyi khrid yig*) is an instruction manual for the practice of uniting one's mind with the spiritual master's, by Payma Gyurmay Gyatso. *The Treasury of Rediscovered Teachings*, Volume 5, pages 289-306.

The Rain of Wisdom (*mchog gi dngos grub mngon du byed pa'i myur lam bka' brgyud bla ma rnams kyi rdo rje'i mgur dbyangs ye shes char 'bebs rang grol lhun grub bde chen rang 'bar nges don rgya mtsho'i snying po*) compiled by the eighth Tai Situpa, Chökyi Jungnay. Translated into English by the Nalanda Translation Committee Translation Committee Translation Committee (Boulder: Shambhala, 1980).

Reciting the Names of Gentle Splendor (*'phags pa 'jam dpal gyi mtshan yang dag par brjod pa*) (K360). Translated into English as *Chanting the Names of Manjushri* by Alex Wayman (Boston: Shambhala, 1985).

Remembering the Three Jewels Discourse (*'phags pa dkon mchog gsum rjes su dran pa'i mdo*) (K279).

The Reunion of Father and Child Discourse (*'phags pa yab sras mjal ba zhes bya ba theg pa chen po'i mdo*) (K60).

The Ritual for the Recitation of The Heart of the Lotus Tantra (*bla ma'i thugs sgrub bar chad kun sel las rang byung bklag pas grol ba padma'i snying po'i rgyud bklag thabs dang cas pa*) by Jamyang Kyentsay Wangpo. *The Treasury of Rediscovered Teachings*, Volume 42, pages 295-302. See also: *The Vajrasattva Practice of Liberation Through Hearing*.

The Ritual of Offering to the Spiritual Masters of the Shangpa Instruction Lineage (*'gro mgon shang pa bka' brgyud kyi bla ma mchod pa'i cho ga yid bzhin nor bu*) by Jamgon Kongtrul. *The Treasury of Precious Instructions of Tibetan Buddhism*, Volume 12, pages 357-88.

The Secret Essence: The Tantra of Illusion (*rgyud thams cad kyi rgyal po dpal sgyu 'phrul rtsa ba'i rgyud gsang ba'i snying po*), published by Tarthang Tulku, Berkeley, 1969.

The Sesame Oil Lamp (*bka' brgyad bde gshegs 'dus pa bsnyen yig til mar sgron me*) is a commentary to the meditation on the Eight Configurations of Deities by Jamgon Kongtrul. *Collected Works*, Volume 4.

The Seven-Line Invocation of Guru Rinpochay (*tsig bdun gsol 'debs*): two are mentioned in this text. The invocation in the tradition of Guru Chöwang is a longer prayer; that in the tradition of Daychen Lingpa is just seven lines long.

The Seven Points of Mind Training (*blo sbyong don bdun ma*) is the "root text" of *The Great Path of Awakening*. See above.

The Seven Prayers (*o rgyan gu ru padma 'byung gnas kyi rdo rje gsung 'khrul pa med pa'i gsol 'debs le'u bdun ma lo rgyus dang cas pa*) were spoken by Guru Rinpochay in response to requests by five of his disciples; discovered by Tulku Zangpo Drakpa, transcribed by Rikzin Godem Chen. *The Treasury of Rediscovered Teachings*, Volume 5, pages 137-86.

The Stages of the Path for the Three Types of Individuals (*rgyal ba'i bstan pa la 'jug pa'i rim pa skyes bu gsum gyi man ngag gi khrid yig bdud rtsi'i nying khu*) by Taranata. *The Treasury of Precious Instructions of Tibetan Buddhism*, Volume 3, pages 181-273.

The Supreme Meditative Absorption Discourse (*'phags pa ting nge 'dzin mchog dam pa*) (K137).

The Tantra of Adamantine Joy (*kye'i rdo rje zhes bya ba rgyud kyi rgyal po*) (K417).

The Tantra of the Glorious Wheel of Time (*mchog gi dang po'i sangs rgyas las phyung ba rgyud kyi rgyal po dpal dus kyi 'khor lo zhes bya ba*) (K362).

The Tantra of Wheel of Supreme Bliss (*dpal bde mchog 'byung ba zhes bya ba'i rgyud kyi rgyal po chen po*) (K373).

The Three-Part Torma Offering (*gtor ma cha gsum gyi cho ga*) is an offering to worldly gods and spirits by Gyurmay Dorjay. *The Treasury of Rediscovered Teachings*, Volume 41, pages 15-22.

The Treasure Vault of Enlightened Activity (*dpal ye shes kyi mgon po phyag drug pa'i sgrub thabs gtor ma'i cho ga dang cas pa phrin las gter mdzod*) is the ritual of offering to Six-Armed Protector by Taranata. *The Treasury of Precious Instructions of Tibetan Buddhism*, Volume 12, pages 573-92.

The Twenty-five Vows (*sdom pa nyer lnga pa*) by Chökyi Wangchuk, included within Kongtrul's *Practices for Periods Between Meditation Sessions* (*thun mtshams rnal 'byor nye bar mkho ba gsar rnying gi gdams ngag snying po bsdus pa dgos pa kun tshang*). *Collected Works*, Volume 12, pages 303-08.

Twenty-one Homages in Praise of Tara (*sgrol ma la phyag tshal nyi shu rtsa gcig gi bstod pa phan yon dang bcas pa*) (K438). Translated into English by Martin Willson as "The Praise in Twenty-One Homages to Our Lady, the Goddess Arya-Tara, with its Benefits," *In Praise of Tara* (London: Wisdom Publications, 1986), pages 113-16.

Twenty Verses on the Bodhisattva Vow (*byang chub sems dpa'i sdom pa nyi shu pa*) by Chandragomin (T4081). Translated into English by Mark Tatz in *Difficult Beginnings* (Boston: Shambhala, 1985).

"Upholding the instructions of Padmakara" (*padmas lung zin*) is a prayer for the long life of Payma Nyinjay Wangpo, the ninth Tai Situpa, by the fourteenth Karmapa, Tekchok Dorjay. It was made into a supplication by its author after Payma Nyinjay's death.

The Vajrasattva Practice of Liberation Through Hearing (*bla ma'i thugs sgrub bar chad kun sel las rigs bdag rdo rje sems dpa'i gsang sngags thos pas grol ba*) by Jamyang Kyentsay Wangpo. *The Treasury of Rediscovered Teachings*, Volume 42, pages 289-302. This text includes *The Ritual for the Recitation of The Heart of the Lotus Tantra* (pages 295-302).

Vermillion (*mtshal ma*). The title written on this text of offering to the protectors of the Oral Instruction Lineage of the Karmapas is *A Torma Offering to the Three Roots and the Guardians of the Doctrine* (*rtsa gsum bka' srung bcas kyi gtor bsngos*). The author of the text is not named; the eighth Tai Situpa, Chökyi Jungnay, wrote the supplication to the lineage at the beginning of the text.

Wish-Fulfilling Ambrosia: The Essential Instructions of Luminosity (*bdud rtsi ljon shing 'od gsal gyi gnad yig*). Text not located.

The Wish-Fulfilling Cobra (*klu gtor gdengs can 'dod 'jo*) is an offering to the nagas by Gyurmay Dorjay. *The Treasury of Rediscovered Teachings*, Volume 28, pages 43-52.

The Wish-Fulfilling Tree of Faith (*dpal ldan bla ma dam pa'i rnam par thar pa dad pa'i ljon shing*) is the autobiographical account in verse of the life of freedom of Taranata. *The Treasury of Precious Instructions of Tibetan Buddhism*, Volume 12, pages 449-52.

Appendix 3
Persons Mentioned in the Retreat Manual

Ananda (*kun dga'o*, "Ever-Joyful") was the Buddha's cousin and one of his closest disciples. He is considered to be one of Kongtrul's previous incarnations.

Atisha (982-1054) is referred to in this text by the nickname Jo-wo (*jo bo*, "Lord"). He was an Indian master whose teachings in Tibet became known there as the Buddha's Word as Instruction Lineage.

Berotsana (Vairochana, "Illuminator of Form") (seventh/eighth century) was one of the principal disciples of Guru Rinpochay. He is considered to be one of Kongtrul's previous incarnations.

Chetsun Sengay Wangchuk (*lche btsun seng ge dbang phyug*, "Noble Tongue, Powerful Lion") (eleventh/twelfth century) was a discoverer of treasure texts who received instructions from Vimalamitra in visions during half a month while he was in retreat. His appearance to Jamyang Kyentsay Wangpo in a vision was the event that produced the instructions called the Profound Essence of Vimalamitra.

Chökyi Jungnay (*chos kyi 'byung gnas*, "Source of Spiritual Instruction") (1700-1775), the eighth Tai Situpa, founded Palpung Monastery.

Chöwang, also called Guru Chöwang; full name is Guru Chökyi Wangchuk (*gu ru chos kyi dbang phyug*, "Lord of Spiritual Life") (1212-1270). Discoverer of the treasure texts including the practice called Quintessential Secret.

Dakpo Rinpochay (*dvaks po rin po che*, "Precious Teacher from Dakpo") is another name for Gampopa.

Daychen Lingpa (*bde chen gling pa*, "Great Bliss"), a treasure revealer of the sixteenth century. Mentioned in this text as the master responsible for the universally popular *Seven-Line Invocation of Guru Rinpochay*.

Dharmashri ("Glorious Spiritual Instructions") (1654-1718) was the brother of Terdak Lingpa and the author of many texts of the Minling tradition of meditation.

Dolpopa or Dolpo Sang-gyay (*dol po sangs rgyas*, "Buddha from Dolpo") (1292-1361) was one of the most outstanding masters of the Vajra Yoga Instruction Lineage.

Drimay Özer (*dri med 'od zer*, "Faultless Light") see Longchen Rabjam Zangpo.

Düdul Dorjay (*bdud 'dul rdo rje*, "Demon-Conquering Vajra") (1733-1797) was the thirteenth Karmapa.

Gampopa (*sgam po pa*, "Person from Gampo") (1079-1153) was the main disciple of Milarepa and the principal instructor of the first Karmapa.

Garwang Chökyi Wangchuk (*gar dbang chos kyi dbang phyug*, "Master of the Dance, Lord of Spiritual Life")(1584-1635) was the sixth Sharmapa.

Guru Rinpochay (*gu ru rin po che*, "Precious Master") was the seventh/eighth-century Indian master who succeeded in firmly establishing tantric Buddhist practice in Tibet.

Humkara (seventh/eighth century) was one of the eight great Indian masters who contributed to the instructions that became the Ancient Instruction Lineage in Tibet.

Jamgon Lama Payma Garwang (*'jam mgon bla ma padma gar dbang*, "Gentle Protector, Lotus Master of the Dance") (1813-1899) was the name Jamgon Kongtrul uses to refer to himself in this text. Payma Garwang was his tantric name.

Jamyang Kyentsay Wangpo (*'jam dbyang mkhyen btse dbang po*, "Soft Melody, Power of Wisdom and Love") (1820-1892) was Kongtrul's teacher, inspiration, and friend.

Jikten Sumgon (*'jig rten gsum mgon*, "Protector of the Three Worlds") (1143-1217) was the originator of the Drigung Kagyu monastic system.

Karma Chakmay (*karma chags med*, "Without Attachment") (1613-1678) was a master whose prolific writings became part of both the Ancient and Oral Instruction Lineages.

Kasyapa (*'od srung*, "Ever-Radiant"), a close disciple of the Buddha, assumed responsibility for the Buddhist community after the Buddha's death.

Kyungpo Naljor (*khyung po rnal 'byor*, "Garuda Yogi") (978-1127) was a Tibetan who travelled a number of times to India in search of instruction in Buddhism. His main spiritual masters were two women, Niguma and Sukasiddhi; his teachings became known in Tibet as the Shangpa Instruction Lineage. He is considered to be one of Kongtrul's previous incarnations.

Longchen Rabjam Zangpo (*klong chen rab 'byams bzang po*, "Infinite Vast Expanse of Excellence") (1318-1363), also known as Longchenpa, was an outstanding scholar and meditation master of the Ancient Instruction Lineage. He is considered to be one of Kongtrul's previous incarnations.

Marpa (*mar pa*) (1012-1096) was a Tibetan who travelled to India in search of Buddhist instruction. His teachings became known in Tibet as the Oral Instruction Lineage of Marpa.

Milarepa (*mi la ras pa*) (1040-1123) was Marpa's principal disciple. Much of his life was spent meditating in caves in western and central Tibet and northern Nepal.

Namkay Nyingpo (*nam mkha'i snying po*, "Heart of the Sky") (seventh/eighth century) was one of the principal disciples of Guru Rinpochay.

Naropa (eleventh century), an Indian scholar-turned-yogi, was the principal teacher of Marpa.

Niguma (eleventh century), either the sister or wife of Naropa, was one of the principal teachers of Kyungpo Naljor.

Orgyen Laytro Lingpa (*o rgyan las phro gling pa*, "Oddiyana, Destined One") (1585-1656) was a discoverer of treasure texts including the practice of the Gathering of the Jewels. Also known as Jatson Nyingpo (*'ja' mtshon snying po*, "Heart of the Rainbow").

Orgyen Terdak Lingpa (*o rgyan gter bdag gling pa*, "Chief of Treasures"), also known as Gyurmay Dorjay (*'gyur med rdo rje*, "Changeless Vajra") (1646-1714), was the founder of the Mindrol Ling monastery and a prolific discoverer of treasure texts. He is considered to be one of Kongtrul's previous incarnations.

Payma Gyurmay Gyatso (*padma 'gyur med rgya mtsho*, "Lotus, Changeless Ocean") (b. late seventeenth century) was the son and a principal disciple of Orgyen Terdak Lingpa.

Payma Nyinjay Wangpo (*padma nyin byed dbang po*, "Lotus, Powerful Sun") (1774-1853), the ninth Tai Situpa, was Kongtrul's principal teacher.

Rangjung Dorjay (*rang 'byung rdo rje*, "Self-Arisen Vajra") (1284-1339) was the third Karmapa.

Sang-gyay Lingpa (*sangs rgyas gling pa*, "Buddha") (1340-1396) was a discoverer of treasure texts, including *The Quintessential Vision of the Spiritual Master*.

Sukasiddhi ("Accomplishment of Bliss") (eleventh century), an Indian woman master, was one of the principal teachers of Kyungpo Naljor.

Tang Tong Gyalpo (*thang stong rgyal po*, "King of the Plain of Emptiness") (1385-1510) was an important figure in many lineages of meditation instruction. He is mentioned in this book as the originator of a style of practice of the Shangpa Instruction Lineage which he received from Niguma.

Taranata (Skt. *taranatha*; Tib. *sgrol ba'i mgon po*, "Liberating Protector") (1575-1634) was an important figure in both the Shangpa Instruction Lineage and the Vajra Yoga Instruction Lineage. He is considered to be one of Kongtrul's previous incarnations.

Tekchok Dorjay (*theg mchog rdo rje*, "Vajra of the Supreme Way") (1797-1845), the fourteenth Karmapa, was one of Kongtrul's teachers.

Terchen Rinpochay (*gter chen rin po che*, "Precious Great Discoverer of Treasures") is the title Kongtrul uses in referring to Chok-gyur Daychen Lingpa (*mchog gyur bde chen gling pa*, "Supreme Great Bliss") (1829-1870), one of Kongtrul's teachers and friends.

Vimalamitra (*dri med bshes gnyen*, "Faultless Spiritual Friend") (seventh/eighth centuries), an Indian master, one of the teachers of Guru Rinpochay who came to Tibet, was one of the eight great Indian masters who contributed to the instructions that became the Ancient Instruction Lineage.

Wangchuk Dorjay (*dbang phyug rdo rje*, "Powerful Vajra") (1556-1603) was the ninth Karmapa.

Yeshay Tsogyal (*ye shes mtsho rgyal*, "Queen of the Lake of Wisdom") (seventh/eighth centuries) was one of the principal disciples of Guru Rinpochay.

Appendix 4
Buddhas, Bodhisattvas, Deities, and Practices Mentioned in the Retreat Manual

Adamantine Joy (Hevajra; Gyaypa Dorjay, *dgyes pa rdo rje*) is a deity of the highest level of tantra within the tantras of the Later Translations.

Black Horse-Neck (Black Hayagriva; Tamdrin Nakpo, *rta mgrin nag po*) is a particularly wrathful form of Horse-Neck, the wrathful deity of the lotus buddha-family within the Eight Great Configurations of Deities.

Black Lord of Life (Tsaydak Nagpo, *tshe bdag nag po*) is a form of Slayer of the Lord of Death (Yamantaka; Shinjay Shay, *gshin rje gshed*), the wrathful deity of the buddha-family within the Eight Great Configurations of Deities.

Buddha Boundless Light (Amitabha; Öpakmay, *'od dpag med*) is the chief of the lotus buddha-family and of the pure land Blissful, where Buddhists of many cultures, including Tibetan, aspire to be reborn.

Buddha of Complete Awareness (Maha-Vairochana; Kun Rik, *kun rig*) is a deity of the first level of tantra within the tantras of the Later Translations.

Consummate King of the Mamos (Mamo Ngondzok Gyalpo, *ma mo mngon rdzogs rgyal po*) is a wrathful deity within the Eight Great Configurations of Deities.

Cutting Through the Solidity of Clinging (Trek Chö, *kregs chod*) is one of the two main divisions of the practice of Great Perfection.

Deathlessness and Non-Entering (of either cyclic existence or perfect peace) (Chimay Chukmay, *'chi med 'chug med*) is the pinnacle of the teachings of the Shangpa Instruction Lineage.

Direct Vision (Tögal, *thod rgal*) is the highest level of practice of Great Perfection.

Eight Great Configurations of Deities (Drubpa Ka Jay, *sgrub pa bka' rgyad*) are meditations on eight configurations of wrathful deities. These practices are the main creation phase meditations of the Ancient Instruction Lineage.

Ever-Excellent (Samantabhadra; Kuntu Zangpo, *kun tu bzang po*) is a name shared by a bodhisattva and a buddha. In this text, Kongtrul refers to the buddha, the highest expression of enlightenment within the system of the Ancient Instruction Lineage.

Five Tantric Deities (Juday Lha Nga, *rgyud sde lha lnga*), a meditation practice within the Shangpa Instruction Lineage, groups five deities of the Highest Yoga Tantra into one meditation.

Gathering of the Jewels (Könchog Chidu, *dkon mchog spyi 'dus*), a treasure teaching discovered by Orgyen Laytro Lingpa, is classified by Kongtrul in *The Treasury of Rediscovered Teachings* as a meditation on the physically manifest body of enlightenment of the peaceful form of Guru Rinpochay.

Gathering of the Joyful Ones of the Eight Great Configurations of Deities (Kajay Daysheg Dupa, *bka' brgyad bde gshegs 'dus pa*), a treasure teaching discovered by Nyang Ral Nyima Özer, is a meditation that includes all of the deities of the Eight Great Configurations of Deities.

Gentle Melody (Manjugosha; Jampay Yang, *'jam pa'i dbyangs*) is another name of Gentle Splendor (Manjushri), one of the eight great bodhisattvas.

Gentle Splendor (Manjushri; Jampal, *'jam dpal*) is one of the eight great bodhisattvas.

Glorious Goddess (Lhamo Palchenmo, *lha mo dpal chen mo*) is apparently a goddess of wealth.

Goddess of Longevity (Tseringma, *tshe ring ma*) is one of the main protectresses of the Himalayan region. She and the four goddesses in her entourage promised to protect Buddhism under the influence of Guru Rinpochay and Milarepa.

Great Perfection (Dzok Chen, *rdzogs chen*) refers to the highest and most direct meditations on the nature of mind transmitted within the Ancient Instruction Lineage.

Great Seal (Mahamudra; Chak-gya Chenpo, *phyag rgya chen po*) refers to the highest and most direct meditations on the nature of mind transmitted within a number of instruction lineages.

Great Seal of the Amulet Box (Chakchen Gau Ma, phyag chen ga'u ma) is the name of a Great Seal practice within the Shangpa Instruction Lineage. It was given this name because Kyungpo Naljor, the Tibetan who received the instructions from Niguma, kept them in an amulet box which he wore around his neck.

Heart-Essence of Longchenpa (Longchen Nyingtig, *klong chen snying thig*) is a treasure teaching discovered by Jigmay Lingpa through three visions he had of Longchenpa. Kongtrul places this text within the section on Ati Yoga in *The Treasury of Rediscovered Teachings*.

Heart-Essence of the Awareness Holders (Rikzin Tuktig, *rig 'dzin thugs thig*), the first treasure teaching discovered by Orgyen Terdak Lingpa, is classified by Kongtrul in *The Treasury of Rediscovered Teachings* as a meditation on the physically manifest body of enlightenment of the peaceful form of Guru Rinpochay.

Heart-Essence of Vimalamitra (Vima Nyingtig, *vi ma snying thig*) is a collecton of teachings on Great Perfection which originated with Vimalamitra, an Indian master who visited Tibet at the time of Guru Rinpochay. This cycle of instructions is transmitted within the Ancient Instruction Lineage.

Heart Practice of Vajrasattva (Dorsem Tuk Kyi Druppa, *rdor sems thugs kyi sgrub pa*) is the name of the Minling practice of Vajrasattva.

Innermost Essence of the Spiritual Master (Lama Yangtig, *bla ma yang thig*) is a series of teachings by Longchenpa on the Heart-Essence of Vimalamitra.

Integrated Practice of the Four Deities (Lha Shi Drildrub, *lha bzhi dril sgrub*) a meditation practice from the Shangpa Instruction Lineage, groups four deities into one meditation. Because the spiritual master is the central figure within the configuration, it is considered to be a practice of union with the mind of the spiritual master.

Lion-Faced Dakini (Singhamukha; Sengay Dongma, *seng ge sdong ma*) is a wrathful feminine expression of enlightenment here mentioned as a form of Guru Rinpochay within the practice of the Gathering of the Jewels.

Lokatri (Drangsong Drimay, *drang srong dri med*) is a fierce form of the bodhisattva Vajra-in-Hand (Vajrapani; Chagna Dorjay, *phyag na rdo rje*).

Loving-Kindness (Maitreya; Jampa, *byams pa*) is one of the eight great bodhisattvas.

Mamo of the Charnel Ground (Dutrö Mamo, *dud khrod ma mo*) is a protectress of the Ancient Instruction Lineage.

Mantra Protectress (Ekajati; Ngag Sungma, *sngag srung ma*) is one of the main protectresses of the Ancient Instruction Lineage.

Peaceful Guru (Guru Shiwa, *gu ru bzhi ba*) is a form of Guru Rinpochay within the practice of the Gathering of the Jewels.

Profound Vital Essence of Vimalamitra (Vimalay Zabtig, *vi ma la'i zab thig*) is a treasure teaching recalled by Jamyang Kyentsay Wangpo at the age of twenty-four. The catalyst for the revelation was a vision he had of Chetsun Sengay Wangchuk. Kongtrul places this text within the section on Ati Yoga in *The Treasury of Rediscovered Teachings*.

Queen of Existence (Sipa Gyalmo, *srid pa rgyal mo*) is a protectress of the Ancient Instruction Lineage.

Quintessential Secret (Sangwa Dupa, *gsang ba 'dus pa*), a treasure teaching discovered by Guru Chöwang, is classified by Kongtrul in *The Treasury of Rediscovered Teachings* as an inner meditation on the ultimate, peaceful form of Guru Rinpochay.

Quintessential Vision of the Spiritual Master (Gongdu, *dgongs 'dus*), a treasure teaching discovered by Sang-gyay Lingpa, is classified by Kongtrul in *The Treasury of Rediscovered Teachings* as a meditation on the physically manifest body of enlightenment of the peaceful form of Guru Rinpochay.

Red Celestial Woman (Red Kachari; Kachö Marmo, *mkha' spyod dmar mo*) is a *dakini* whose meditation forms part of the Shangpa Instruction Lineage.

Secret Vital Essence (Sangtig, *gsang thig*) is a treasure teaching discovered by Chok-gyur Daychen Lingpa in the vicinity of Kongtrul's retreat center. The three practices of this cycle — Vajrasattva, Yangdak, and Vajra Dagger — were performed daily during the retreat.

Severance (Chö, *gcod*) was the sole lineage of practice among the eight practice lineages that flourished in the Himalayan region to have originated in Tibet. The woman who developed it was Ma Chik Labdron.

Shakyamuni (Shakya Tupa, *shakya thub pa*; "Sage of the Shakyas") was the historical buddha.

Six-Armed Protector (Mahakala; Chak Drukpa, *phyag drug pa*) is a protector whose practices originally travelled from India to the Tibetan-speaking world through Kyungpo Naljor and the Shangpa Instruction Lineage. It has since become one of the most widely practiced protectors.

Six Branches of Application (Jorwa Yenlak Druk, *sbyor ba yan lag drug*) are the completion phase meditations of the Vajra Yoga Instruction Lineage.

Six Doctrines of Niguma (Nigu Chö Druk, *ni gu chos drug*) are a set of six meditations that Niguma received directly from the Buddha Vajra Holder. These form the root of the Shangpa Instruction Lineage.

Six Doctrines of Sukasiddhi (Suka Chö Druk, *su kha chos drug*) are a set of six meditations that Sukasiddhi received directly from the Buddha Vajra Holder. These form part of the Shangpa Instruction Lineage.

Son of Renown (Vaishravana; Namtosay, *rnam thos sras*) is a wealth god and guardian of the northern direction.

Swift-Acting Fully Awakened Protector (Nyur Dzay Yeshay Kyi Gonpo, *myur mdzad ye shes kyi mgon po*) is another name for Six-Armed Protector.

Tara (Drolma, *grol ma*; "She Who Liberates") is a bodhisattva who has vowed to always be born as a female and to equal the enlightened activity of all buddhas.

Three Meditations-in-Action (Lam Kyer Nam Sum, *lam khyer rnam gsum*) is the meditation practice that follows Great Seal within the Shangpa Instruction Lineage.

Three Yellow Deities (Serpo Kor Sum, *ser po skor gsum*) are three wealth gods, all yellow in color: Son of Renown, Yellow Jambhala, and Goddess of Continual Wealth (Lhamo Nor Gyunma, *lha mo nor rgyun ma*).

Trokma (*'phrog ma*) is a harmful spirit who was put under oath by the Buddha. In return for her promise not to harm human beings, she receives a daily portion of food from ordained persons.

Unshakable Buddha (Akshobya; Mitrukpa, *mi 'khrug pa*) is chief of the vajra buddha-family.

Vajra Black-Caped One (Dorjay Bernak Chen, *rdo rje ber nag can*) is the principal protector of the Karmapas.

Vajra Dagger (Vajra Kilaya; Dorjay Purba, *rdo rje phur ba*) is the wrathful deity of the karma buddha-family within the Eight Great Configurations of Deities. The dagger he bears is three-sided.

Vajra Holder (Vajradhara; Dorjay Chang, *rdo rje 'chang*) is the form in which the Buddha appeared when teaching tantra.

Vajrasattva (Dorjay Sempa, *rdo rje sems dpa'*) is one of the principal buddhas of tantric Buddhism.

Vajra Youth (Dorjay Shunnu, *rdo rje gzhun nu*) is another name for Vajra Dagger.

Vital Essence of Liberation (Drol Tig, *grol tig*) is a treasure teaching discovered by Drodul Lingpa.

Wheel of Supreme Bliss (Chakrasamvara; Korlo Demchok, *'khor lo bde mchog*) is a deity of the highest level of tantra within the tantras of the Later Translations.

Wheel of Time (Kalachakra; Dukyi Korlo, *dus kyi 'khor lo*) is the deity whose meditation represents the pinnacle of the tantras of the Later Translations.

White Celestial Woman (White Kachari; Kachö Karmo, *mkha' spyod dkar mo*) is a *dakini* whose meditation forms part of the Shangpa Instruction Lineage.

White Tara (Drolkar, *grol dkar*) or Wish-Fulfilling Wheel (Yishin Korlo, *yid bzhin 'khor lo*) is the form of Tara who bestows longevity and wisdom.

Wrathful Guru (Guru Drakpo, *gu ru drak po*) is the secret form of Guru Rinpochay within the practice of the Gathering of the Jewels.

Yangdak Heruka (*yang dag he ru ka*) is the wrathful deity of the vajra buddha-family within the Eight Great Configurations of Deities.

Index

A

B

C

D

H

I

Q

R

Y

Z